HYRUM LEWIS, PhD

THERE IS A GOD

HOW TO RESPOND TO ATHEISM IN THE LAST DAYS

CFI,
AN IMPRINT OF CEDAR FORT, INC.
SPRINGVILLE, UTAH

FOR DALLAS

ISBN 13: 978-1-4621-2041-3

Published by CFI, an imprint of Cedar Fort, Inc.,
2373 W. 700 S., Springville, UT 84663
Distributed by Cedar Fort, Inc., www.cedarfort.com

LIBRARY OF CONGRESS CATALOGING-IN-PUBLICATION DATA ON FILE

Names: Lewis, Hyrum S. (Hyrum Smith), author.
Title: There is a God : how to respond to atheism in the last days / by Hyrum
   Lewis.
Description: Springville, UT : CFI, an imprint of Cedar Fort, Inc., [2017] |
   Includes bibliographical references and index.
Identifiers: LCCN 2017006889 (print) | LCCN 2017012625 (ebook) | ISBN
   9781462127962 | ISBN 9781462120413 (pbk. : alk. paper)
Subjects: LCSH: Church of Jesus Christ of Latter-day Saints--Apologetic
   works. | Church of Jesus Christ of Latter-day Saints--Doctrines. | Mormon
   Church--Doctrines. | Christianity and atheism. | Apologetics.
Classification: LCC BX8635.5 (ebook) | LCC BX8635.5 .L49 2017 (print) | DDC
   230/.9332--dc23
LC record available at https://lccn.loc.gov/2017006889

Cover design by Shawnda T. Craig
Cover design © 2017 by Cedar Fort, Inc.

Printed in the United States of America

10 9 8 7 6 5 4 3 2 1

Printed on acid-free paper

CONTENTS

INTRODUCTION

A THEISM HAS BEEN ON THE rise in America in recent decades. Anti-religion books have become best sellers, the culture has become increasingly secular, and religious affiliation has declined among the population.[1] Unfortunately, Latter-day Saints haven't been immune to this trend. Many Mormons have concluded that God doesn't exist and have left the Church, while others sit on the fence, clinging to their faith with fear and apprehension, as evidence against the existence of God seems to mount.[2] Elder Robert D. Hales recently warned, "We live in a time when the darkness of secularism is deepening around us. Belief in God is widely

---

1   See Paul Taylor, The Next America (NY: Public Affairs, 2014); Douglas Main, "Study: America Becoming Less Christian, More Secular," *Newsweek,* May 12, 2015; and Phil Zuckerman, "Christianity Declining, Secularism Rising," *Psychology Today*, May 12, 2015. Fifteen years ago, after a disaster it was standard to say, "Our prayers are with the victims." Now it's more customary to say, "Our thoughts go out to the victims." The increasing vulgarity, permissiveness, and crassness in America are also evidence of the decline in religious values.

2   There is no reason to think that the recent trend toward secularism is inevitable or irreversible. Over the course of American history, there have been periods of religious decline and periods of religious revival, such as the awakenings of the 1740s, 1820s, and 1950s. Overall, the general trend from Jamestown to the present has been increasing religiosity. See Roger Finke and Rodney Stark, *The Churching of America, 1776–1990* (New Brunswick: Rutgers University Press, 2005); and Jon Butler, *Awash in a Sea of Faith: Christianizing the American People* (Cambridge: Harvard University Press, 1992). We have every reason to expect yet another religious awakening at some point. Many find this claim strange but only because of our human tendency to project recent trends indefinitely into the future. For example, in the 1990s, the growth of free markets seemed the inevitable path of the future, but it has now been halted and reversed worldwide. The same may eventually be true of secularism.

questioned and even attacked in the name of political, social, and even religious causes."[3]

The purpose of this book is to equip Latter-day Saints with tools to understand and answer the atheist attacks that they will inevitably encounter during their lives. Strengthening ourselves against secular arguments is an important part of defending against the "fiery darts of the adversary" in the last days (1 Nephi 15:24). By addressing atheism on an intellectual level and from a gospel perspective, members of the Church can reinforce their own testimonies and perhaps even help bring back those who have strayed.

Some might claim that you don't get far when using intellect in matters of testimony and that it is much better to rely on spiritual witness. However, the scriptures encourage us to seek learning by study *and* faith (see D&C 88:118). Heart and mind work together in the pursuit of truth. Without both, our testimonies are not as robust as they could be.[4] Isaiah counseled us, "Come now, and let us reason together," (1:18), suggesting that God doesn't only permit us to use our intellectual faculties in religious matters; rather, He commands it.

Nevertheless, members of the Church may cluster into one camp or the other. Some may focus on only the "study" half of the equation, believing that scholarship can prove the Church is true (for example, through Book of Mormon evidences), not realizing that evidence for the gospel is only convincing to those already inclined through faith to accept it. *Study needs faith*.

Other members may only accept the "faith" half of the equation, claiming we don't need to use our minds in religious matters because the Spirit alone is sufficient for a testimony. This may be true for many in the Church but not for all. Without reason and evidence, skeptics will dismiss spiritual experiences as "just feelings" foisted on them by evolution-produced brain wiring. I know of dozens of cases in which people left

---

3   Robert D. Hales, "Seeking to Know God, Our Heavenly Father, and His Son, Jesus Christ," *Ensign*, November 2009.

4   Apostle John A. Widtsoe, an agricultural scientist, would often find answers to his scientific questions while sitting in the temple (Truman G. Madsen, "The Temple and the Atonement," abridged from a lecture delivered in Saratoga, California, 16 October 1994, accessed December 15, 2016, publications.mi.byu .edu/publications/transcripts/I00066-The_Temple_and_the_Atonement.html).

the Church, claiming they only *thought* they had felt the Spirit but now understood that science explains away those feelings as illusions. Because even spiritual experiences can be set aside when not rationally justified, intellectual arguments for faith can be crucial, especially for those of a skeptical disposition. Reason in the context of faith can strengthen and protect testimony. *Faith needs study.*

Together, study and faith constitute the two pillars that hold up a testimony.[5] My hope is that this book can help with the study pillar, which will, in turn, strengthen the faith pillar. Of course, I encourage everyone to seek spiritual witnesses and to live the gospel, but I also encourage them to read this book with the hope that its reasoning can accompany and bolster their faith.

Before we begin, I offer a few disclaimers. I was trained as a historian and only minored in philosophy at the doctoral level. Although I'm not equipped to do the technical work of professional philosophers, I like to think I have enough familiarity with the basic ideas of history's great thinkers to engage their central arguments. Most of what atheists promote these days can't stand up to even minor scrutiny, and common sense reasoning can make this clear.

With this approach, I'm engaging the atheists on their own terms. They write popular books for common readers, not academic treatises for the theologically sophisticated. In the following pages, I respond in kind. To the charge that these arguments are broad, non-academic, and wanting nuance, I respond: so are those of the New Atheists. My lack of citation and, perhaps, originality will likely disappoint many scholars, but they are not my intended audience. Thoughtful lay members of the Church are. Just as one need not have a PhD in math to know that 2 + 2 does not equal 5, so one need not have a PhD in science to know that matter does not make mind.[6]

---

5   Elder M. Russell Ballard emphasized the need for both pillars in his recent talk, "By Study and Faith," *Liahona*, December 2016.

6   Although some might see this popular approach as a problem, experience has taught me that common sense is often preferable to academic scholarship when it comes to fundamental, nonscientific issues. This preference is borne out in a number of studies, such as James Surowiecki's *The Wisdom of Crowds* (NY: Knopf, 2005); and Philip Tetlock's *Expert Political Judgment* (Princeton: Princeton University Press, 2009). Of course, there is a place for experts, but generally on matters that are empirically verifiable (knowable through the senses), such as determining the mass

And if people can be turned *to* atheism through common sense reasoning (by reading Richard Dawkins, for instance), then they should be
able to be turned *from* it in the same way.[7] Latter-day Saints don't believe
in a God who would only make Himself known to intellectual elites. Just
as everyone can understand the truths of the Declaration of Independence, so can everyone understand the reasons for God's existence.

We can also assume that deferring to the experts on these issues is not
only undesirable, but is in fact impossible, since the experts have widely
differing views among themselves. Unlike matters of, say, chemistry, where
everyone agrees on the basic facts (that helium has an atomic number of
two or that water boils at 100 degrees Celsius), questions of free will, materialism, and ethics are widely debated, and there is no expert consensus to
defer to.[8] Because of this, sound, basic reasoning can be far preferable to the
latest scholarship. To their credit, most of the New Atheists would agree.[9]

---

of the earth or the efficacy of antibiotics in curing disease. On matters that are not
scientific—such as moral, philosophical, political, or religious truths—I've found
that common people are generally more trustworthy than intellectuals who are often
blinded by arrogance and insularity. As evidence, consider that NYU physicist Alan
Sokal proved conclusively that a large portion of humanities scholarship is, quite
literally, absurd. Professor Sokal submitted a fake article (generously peppered with
typical high-sounding postmodern shibboleths) to one of the top literary journals
in the country, Duke University's *Social Text*, arguing that the law of gravity was a
"social construction." Unbelievably, the article was accepted for publication. (See
Paul A. Boghossian, "What the Sokal Hoax Ought to Teach Us: The Pernicious
Consequences and Internal Contradictions of 'Postmodernist' Relativism," *Times
Literary Supplement*, December 13, 1996, 14–15.)

7   Just as it's unfair to say that Dawkins is not a theologian and therefore his
     arguments have no merit (Terry Eagleton, "Lunging, Flailing, Mispunching,"
     London Review of Books vol. 28, no. 20, [October 19, 2006], 32–34), so I believe
     it's unfair to say that Lewis is not a theologian and therefore the arguments in this
     book have no merit.

8   Expert disagreement on fundamental issues is visible in such collections as John
     Brockman, ed., *This Idea Must Die: Scientific Theories That Are Blocking Progress*
     (NY: HarperCollins, 2015), where an expert on one page will declare a certain
     idea dead (for example, determinism) and an expert on the next page will declare
     the opposite idea dead (for example, indeterminism). When expert opinion is so
     radically divided, it is impossible to defer to a consensus of experts.

9   See, for instance, Steven Weinberg, "Sokal's Hoax," *The New York Review
     of Books* vol. 43, no. 13, (August 8, 1996), 11–15; and Richard Dawkins,

The following chapters will help expose the weaknesses of the atheist position in light of the gospel and will aid us all in seeking and trusting spiritual witnesses of the truth. This book is an extended personal reflection on religion—more essay than monograph—and a justification of my beliefs that others may profit from. It addresses the standard claims of atheism and explains why I, through the restored gospel, have come down strongly on the side of belief in God. I am sharing what has helped me on my own journey of faith, and I hope it can help others on theirs.

Finally, this book was not necessarily meant to be read sequentially. The chapters are organized to introduce unfamiliar terms, but readers should feel free to go directly to those chapters they feel are most relevant or interesting. I believe that chapters four and five contain some of the strongest arguments against atheism. I encourage readers who may not complete the whole book to go to those chapters first.

Hyrum Lewis
Stanford, California
January 2017

"Postmodernism Disrobed," *Nature*, vol. 394 (July 1998), 141–43. There is value in postmodernism when it helps us recognize our limitations (as we shall see later), but too much of it is used to justify an extreme relativism that invalidates all knowledge claims.

A NOTE ON TERMINOLOGY AND TONE

In this book, I will use the term *atheist* in its most basic sense, meaning "someone who doesn't believe there is a God." Many, if not most, atheists might technically be termed *agnostic*, in that they don't know for sure that God does not exist. Even Richard Dawkins, the world's leading atheist, only says, "There is *almost certainly* no God"[10]—but since they call themselves atheists, I will use that term as well.[11]

The most prominent of the self-identified New Atheists today are the Four Horsemen of atheism: Richard Dawkins, Christopher Hitchens, Daniel Dennett, and Sam Harris. Because I am responding to a composite of these four atheists and their confreres, as well as to the many atheists I have personally interacted with, I won't always cite specific passages from their works.[12] I share Elder Holland's view that these figures are only stars in a "dim firmament,"[13] and that although they may appear profound on the surface, they are superficial deep down—a point this book should make clear.

Underlying the New Atheism of today is the philosophy of materialist-empiricism.[14] The "materialist" part of the philosophy says

---

10   "Why There Is Almost Certainly No God" is the title of chapter four of Dawkins's book, *The God Delusion* (Boston: Houghton Mifflin, 2006); emphasis added.

11   The word *atheist* is also appropriate since the atheist disbelief in God is about as certain as the belief in God of the religious. It goes beyond the agnostic's claim of not knowing and goes toward the confidence most of us have about the nonexistence of the tooth fairy.

12   Most prominent of their works are Dawkins, *The God Delusion*, Sam Harris, *The End of Faith* (NY: Norton, 2005), Daniel Dennett, *Breaking the Spell* (NY: Penguin, 2006), and Christopher Hitchens, *God Is Not Great* (NY: Hachette, 2007). Their confreres include comedian Bill Maher, journalist Michael Shermer, and physicist Steven Weinberg.

13   Jeffrey R. Holland, "Bound by Loving Ties," (2016 BYU Campus Education Week devotional, Provo, Utah, August 16, 2016).

14   Many thinkers today prefer the more expansive term "physicalism," but "materialism" is the more common term and is sufficient for our purposes.

that only matter exists.[15] The "empiricism" part says that sensory experience, and only sensory experience, can provide knowledge—i.e. "seeing is believing."[16] In the materialist-empiricist view, if we refer to anything such as spirit, God, free will, or mind, we are, quite literally speaking nonsense.[17] In this book, I challenge the New Atheism by opposing the materialist-empiricism on which it is based. Although atheism and materialist-empiricism are not exactly synonyms, they can fairly be treated as such, since the unseen, nonmaterial realm is that of spirit, heaven, angels, God, and all else that the atheist philosophy, at its very core, denies.[18]

I also recognize that the world is full of many good-hearted atheists. They don't believe in God but are civil in dialogue and respectful of beliefs they don't share. They have legitimate concerns, such as God's invisibility or the prevalence of heartbreak and evil in a world supposedly created by a benevolent God. When I use the term *atheist*, I am not referring to these individuals but only to the cavalier, rude, insulting, and intolerant New Atheists, such as Richard Dawkins. Among other

---

15 Doctrine and Covenants 131:7–8 suggests a kind of spiritual materialism in which even spirit is a type of matter: "There is no such thing as immaterial matter. All spirit is matter, but it is more fine or pure." But this spiritual materialism still recognizes an unseen level of matter and the reality of nonmaterial intelligence. It therefore suggests a kind of dualism in the universe and is quite different from the materialism of the atheists. We might, then, speak of a two-level materialism (that of D&C 131) and a one-level materialism (that of the atheists). Obviously, this book challenges only the one-level materialism.

16 In the most general sense, empiricism means that the senses are *a* path to knowledge, but the empiricism of the atheists is more narrow and says that the senses are the *only* path to knowledge. I use the term "empiricism" here for convenience, even though narrow empiricism or exclusionary empiricism might be more accurate since we Latter-day Saints are empiricists in the broader sense of the term.

17 For a good summary of materialist-empiricism (often used as a synonym with naturalism), see Dawkins, *The God Delusion*, 34–35.

18 Ibid. Even so, not all atheists are empiricists or materialists. Novelist Ayn Rand, for instance, was notably anti-materialist—somehow affirming the spirit of man while denying the existence of God—but since atheistic nonmaterialism is especially incoherent and rare, I will treat materialism and atheism as generally synonymous in this book. See Ayn Rand, *The Romantic Manifesto* (NY: Penguin, 1971); and Ayn Rand, interview with Phil Donahue in the documentary film, *Ayn Rand: A Sense of Life* (1997).

things, Dawkins has said that Mormon beliefs are "frankly bonkers" and that Mormons are so gullible they should be disqualified from holding public office. He has also said that any parent teaching religion to a child is guilty of child abuse.[19] In this book, I've tried to aim for a higher tone, but I have not always been successful. The New Atheists behave like intellectual bullies, and perhaps there is some merit in standing up to them on their own terms. I hope readers will forgive my occasional descent to their level of discourse.[20]

---

19   Dawkins, "Banishing the Green-Eyed Monster," *The Washington Post Online*, November 2007, accessed July 22, 2009, available from: newsweek.washingtonpost .com/onfaith/panelists/richard_dawkins/2007/11/banishing_the_greeneyed _monste.html; and Dawkins, *The God Delusion*, chapter 9.

20   I also hope readers will be able to present these arguments to doubters in a more conciliatory and loving way than I have been able to. Conveying a combative tone in writing is a weakness I am still working to overcome.

Chapter 1

THE ARGUMENT FROM EVIL

We begin with one of the most powerful, common, and convincing of atheist arguments—the argument from evil. It goes like this: God can't exist because an all-powerful, all-righteous God would not allow the evil and suffering that are so prevalent in the world. What kind of deity would permit the nearly endless catalog of disease, torture, heartbreak, oppression, genocide, war, famine, sickness, hopelessness, and disaster that we find throughout human history? If God really loves His children, why wouldn't He stop all of this evil with a wave of His all-powerful hand?[1] This leads many sincere people (especially in times of hardship) to conclude that God must not exist.

MYSTERY

Because the argument from evil is pervasive and poses a serious challenge to belief, theologians have developed an entire field—theodicy—to address it. A common response to the argument from evil, especially coming from those of mainstream Christian denominations, is an appeal to mystery. They say that we don't know all of God's reasoning, and an infinitely knowledgeable and powerful being who has our best interests in mind may not be comprehensible to limited, sinful beings like us (see Romans 11:33–34). In other words, some humility is in order. Our faith in God could demand a holy surrender on our part.

---

1   This argument is well expressed in Sam Harris, *Letter to a Christian Nation* (NY: Knopf, 2006), 13–16.

We may simply have to accept that God's ways are not our ways (see Isaiah 55:8–9).[2]

However, invoking mystery and leaving it at that may look like a dodge to our atheist friends.[3] Do we have something better? Latter-day Saints do. While we may be stuck with "mystery" as a final answer to many profound questions about God's nature, LDS theology gives us a unique view of suffering that helps us understand how the existence of evil is compatible with the reality of God.

CREATIVE DESTRUCTION

Among the most important insights that the gospel provides is a recognition of the *necessary link between growth and suffering*. As Latter-day Saints, the goal of our existence, the central purpose of this life, and God's own "work and glory" is to bring about our progress toward eternal life (see Moses 1:39). If this progress is the whole point of mortality and if it requires suffering, then suffering is inevitably bound up with the purpose of life. When we understand this basic fact about God and ourselves, we come to this profound truth: *God will allow suffering if it furthers our progress*. Suffering is therefore baked into the plan of salvation.

Our suffering doesn't come because God wants us to hurt but because He wants us to grow. Suffering is the price we pay for progress, and we agreed to this trade-off in our premortal existence. The slogan "no pain, no gain" is actually an eternal principle. The end goal for us (or God) is not the pain but the gain.

We might compare this LDS answer to the problem of evil to economist Joseph Schumpeter's conception of "creative destruction."[4] Just as destruction is necessary for progress in technology, biology, medicine,

---

2   For a popular presentation of this argument, see Michael Novak, *No One Sees God* (NY: Doubleday, 2008).

3   Other traditions claim that evil isn't real but is instead an illusion, something that has no positive reality, but is simply the absence of good. Under this view, God didn't create evil, but an absence of His goodness is what we experience as suffering and evil.

4   First introduced in his work *Capitalism, Socialism, and Democracy*, 3rd ed., (NY: Harper and Brothers, 1950), 83.

politics, business, and all other fields, destruction is necessary for progress in spiritual matters as well.[5] What is repentance if not a piece-by-piece destruction of our old self and the creative building of a new, more righteous self? God commands repentance because He wants to destroy us; that is, He wants to destroy the old us in order to rebuild a new, better us.

So profound is this destruction that covenants are designed to make us think in terms of a new, renewed person born again through Christ. In Mosiah 5:2, the Nephites declared that they had experienced "a mighty change" such that they had "no more disposition to do evil, but to do good continually." We even take upon ourselves a new name to reflect our new identity (see D&C 130:11 and Revelation 2:17). A man named Abram made covenants and became Abraham. A man named Simon made covenants and became Peter. A man named Jacob made covenants and became Israel. The idea of destroying the old self to become a "new man" is found throughout the scriptures (see John 3:3 and Colossians 3:9–10). We sometimes compare repentance to an eraser that removes sin, but we should also liken it to a staircase that lifts. We rise as we make the effort of taking each step.

Isaiah speaks of God building with "hewn stones" (Isaiah 9:10). If a block of stone could talk while under the chisel of a skilled mason, it would likely complain of the pounding and distress, not realizing that it was being fashioned into a masterpiece. C. S. Lewis taught of God knocking down the walls of a house in the process of constructing a palace.[6] Apostle Hugh B. Brown told of cutting down the excess branches of a currant bush so that it could bring forth fruit.[7] All of these metaphors teach the reality of spiritual creative destruction.

Critics of biblical religion often point to Old Testament scriptures that tell of God commanding the destruction of entire societies. To atheists, this destruction is something to mock (God is a genocidal maniac, say the

---

5   Renowned LDS business guru Clayton Christensen made a powerful case for disruption as a spur to economic and technological progress in his influential book *The Innovator's Dilemma* (Cambridge: Harvard Business Review Press, 1997).

6   C. S. Lewis, *Mere Christianity* (Grand Rapids, MI: Zondervan, 2001), 205.

7   Hugh B. Brown, "The Currant Bush," *The New Era,* January 1973.

New Atheists[8]), while believers often squirm uncomfortably at the mention of these scriptures and do their best to avoid them.[9] But if we understand the role that destruction plays in the gospel, many of these passages can be instructive rather than bothersome. Notice that periods of happiness, peace, and utopia, when God has built a near-perfect people, were almost always preceded by terrible destruction. The death and devastation in Canaan was followed by the establishment of Israel in the promised land. The wars and seismic calamities of 3 Nephi were followed by the utopian harmony of 4 Nephi. The Saints' violent expulsion from Jackson County was followed by the spiritual Pentecost and social unity that accompanied the Kirtland Temple dedication (compare D&C 101 to 109 and 110). Destruction, for God, is creative rather than vindictive in nature.

This also applies on an individual level. Destructive suffering nearly always accompanies personal spiritual growth. Nephi was forced out of his homeland, severely beaten, threatened by his brothers, and forced to wander for years in a harsh wilderness. But then came the payoff: the Lord took him into a high mountain, showed him the coming of the Son of God, and gave him an all-encompassing, panoramic vision of the world and its future (see 1 Nephi 11–15).

In the Pearl of Great Price, we read of Abraham going through the harrowing experience of nearly being sacrificed to false gods by his own father (see Abraham 1–2). Only after this did he receive the overpowering view of God's creations found in Abraham 3–5.

In the Old Testament, we read of Daniel suffering political oppression at the hands of the Babylonians because of his faith, but afterward receiving one of the greatest visions of pre-Christian times. In the New Testament, we read that the Apostle Paul was shipwrecked, beaten, and imprisoned, but in the wake of this suffering he received the inspiration to write much of the New Testament.

Joseph Smith faced opposition from the First Vision onward. Thieves, bullies, and bigots attacked him and never let up until his death in Carthage Jail. And yet, accompanying this suffering were the greatest revelatory manifestations of the last days. Brigham Young was driven out of his

---

8   See, for instance, Dawkins, *The God Delusion*, 269–81; and Hitchens, *God Is Not Great*, chapter 7.

9   Latter-day Saints might even attribute these passages to the mistranslations and errors that we believe have crept into the biblical text over the millennia.

Nauvoo home with the other Saints but then received the revelation that became his contribution to modern-day scripture—"The Word and Will of the Lord" (see D&C 136). Joseph F. Smith lost multiple children to tragic deaths. Only after enduring this heartbreak was he given the vision of heaven that has become Doctrine and Covenants 138. Thousands of people in the world today have had personal visions of Christ, yet they had to pass through death itself (near-death experiences) to have that privilege.

To the skeptic who asks why they can't see God, the correct answer may be that they don't want to. Great spiritual witness is usually accompanied by great suffering, and only the most spiritually advanced are willing to pay that price. Those who want to be spared pain may also be spared the spiritual growth and experience that can go along with it.

Not only is suffering bound up with our growth, but it is also bound up with our ability to experience joy. All things have their opposite, and we can only understand the thesis (pleasure) if we also experience the antithesis (pain). Atheists rail against a God who would allow us to die, but how could we ever appreciate eternal life if we never experienced mortality and the certainty of death? How could we ever appreciate health without ever being sick? How could we appreciate water without feeling thirst?

As a college professor, I've come to understand God's perspective in a more personal way. I'm happy to help my students prepare for their exams, but I can't just give them the answers. To do so would thwart their learning. My students probably think I'm being cruel by withholding the answers and requiring them to struggle with the course material, but it is for their own growth. There is intense effort (even pain) in preparing for a test, but without it there can be no learning, no intellectual accomplishment, and no joy in the achievement of a high grade.

If I won't give my students the solutions to their test questions, then that gives us a glimpse into why God won't give us the solutions to war, disease, disaster, and poverty. If life is a test to help us learn, then our suffering is part of that learning. An all-powerful God could do away with our afflictions, but only at the price of our progress. As my wife reminds me often, "God cares more about our growth than our comfort." Suffering is not purposeless; it is creative and helps us move toward our eternal goals. Once we understand this, many of the objections to God's existence disappear.

LIBERTY JAIL REVELATIONS

Sections 121 and 122 of the Doctrine and Covenants, given during the Prophet Joseph Smith's confinement in Liberty Jail, contain four of the most profound responses to the problem of evil ever given. First, the Lord made clear that Joseph Smith was not alone in suffering innocently, for no matter how terrible his afflictions, "the Son of Man hath descended below them all" (D&C 122:8). This summarizes one of Christianity's great answers to the problem of evil. Before asking, "God, how You could do that to You?" You must first ask the far more difficult question: "God, how could You do this to You?" Christ has suffered everything we have suffered and more. We might be comforted to know that He is not an aloof deity watching our pain with indifference. He experiences our trials with us, in all of their intensity and tangibility. He understands severe grief, anxiety, depression, disease, wanting, longing, temptation, hunger, thirst, loneliness, and pain because He suffered it all Himself in Gethsemane, on Golgotha, and in His everyday life. He who deserved suffering the least suffered the most.

The Lord also consoled the Prophet Joseph by reminding him that his friends (at least most of them) still stood by him (see D&C 121:9). The Prophet had a burden almost too great to bear, but God provided him with others who could help shoulder it. Moses had a similar experience. The Lord told him, "I will take of the spirit which is upon thee, and will put it upon [the seventy men of the elders of Israel] and they shall bear the burden of the people with thee, that thou bear it not thyself alone" (Numbers 11:17). In our trials, do we recognize that, while God may not remove the trial, He will often send others to help us through?

God also reminded Joseph of the principle of redemptive suffering. It may have been hard for the Prophet to hear, and it remains hard for us to hear today, but it is profound: "Know thou, my son, that all these things shall give thee experience, and shall be for thy good" (D&C 122:7). The purpose of life, contrary to what the atheists tell us, is not to maximize pleasure and avoid suffering but to become ennobled, glorified, and sanctified. If this requires pain to accomplish, we must submit to this, "even as a child doth submit to his father" (Mosiah 3:19). A two-year-old receiving a vaccine shot might wonder how their parent could be so cruel, but the wise parent understands that the long-term health of the child demands the short-term pain.

Finally, the Lord assured Joseph that his suffering, which seemed overwhelming at the time, would someday appear as "but a small moment" (D&C 121:7). When this mortal life is over, we will look back and realize that what seemed like never-ending torment was actually comparatively brief. Joseph spent six miserable months confined in a cramped, freezing, filthy dungeon called Liberty Jail. Looking back now, the Prophet doubtless remembers those six months as next to nothing. This life is just a blink of an eye in the eternal perspective. Our suffering, no matter how great, may turn out to be less overwhelming than it currently appears. God will allow our *temporary* suffering to achieve our *eternal* good.

FREE WILL

The Latter-day Saint emphasis on freedom of will also makes our theology robust against the argument from evil. Other Christian denominations believe that God created us and our universe *ex nihilo*, but we Latter-day Saints are almost alone in believing that God did not create the intelligence from which our spirits were formed; therefore, He respects our autonomous will even if we abuse it and thereby cause suffering (see D&C 93).[10] Human choices explain much (perhaps most) of the suffering in the world. The unrighteous choices of political leaders, not the will of God, created the two world wars, Hitler's genocide, Mao's famine, Stalin's oppression, and many other major horrors of the twentieth century.

It's also true that much of our own individual suffering is the result of our poor choices. Choosing indolence can lead to poverty, choosing selfishness can lead to loneliness, choosing to ignore the Word of Wisdom can lead to addictions, and so on. God could not stop that suffering without depriving us of our agency. Like the Nephites who prospered when they were more righteous and suffered when they were more wicked, most Latter-day Saints would attest to seeing greater peace, prosperity, and happiness in their own lives when they are choosing to obey the commandments. Since human choices can bring suffering, suffering is the price of agency.

GOD'S LIMITS

Mormons can also answer the problem of evil by understanding that God is bound by his own nature. Notice that the atheist argument from

---

10 Neal A. Maxwell, "Swallowed up in the Will of the Father," *Ensign*, November 1995.

evil isn't really an argument against God but only against *a certain kind* of God—an all-powerful and all-good one.[11] My guess is that atheists know by intuition that God must be good and powerful, so their refutation of a certain kind of god presupposes a knowledge of that god's characteristics and, therefore, his existence. Perhaps they are not arguing so much *against* God, but arguing *with* God (as many of us have done from time to time) for allowing suffering.

While Mormons do believe in an all-powerful God, we must be clear on what that means. Truman Madsen pointed out that God can do impossible things but not "com-possible" things. God, for instance, can't love us and *not* love us at the same time, nor create a rock that is too heavy for Him to lift. Nor, the scriptures tell us, can God allow mercy to rob justice (see Alma 42:25). God, in other words, is limited by His own godliness. We believe in God's omnipotence but only to the degree that it is consonant with His nature.

Understanding the correct meaning of "all-powerful" eliminates the core of the atheist argument for evil. Could God remove all of our suffering and still achieve His purposes? Apparently not. This does not rob Him of His omnipotence but only shows that He would be at odds with His own nature if He defied this principle.

CIRCULARITY

There is also a certain circularity in the argument from evil. I recently heard an atheist say, "How could a loving God watch terminally ill children suffer in a hospital when He could instantly bring an end to their torment and make them happy and healed?" From an LDS point of view, the answer is simple: *He will.* When those children die, they will be relieved of all suffering, return to God, and have more happiness and healing than we can imagine. But to an atheist who rejects the idea that death is a transition to a higher realm of existence, this answer is unsatisfactory: there is no God and no afterlife so death is a terrible, final, ultimate evil. And

---

11   Amateur theologians such as diplomat George Kennan and novelist Norman Mailer have even suggested that God is neither all good nor all powerful. Kennan posited a "higher God" who created the universe with all of its evil, and a "lower God"—Jesus Christ—who helps us combat that evil (Kennan, *Around the Cragged Hill: A Personal and Political Philosophy* [NY: Norton, 1993]). Mailer believed that God was a creator but also a trickster who liked to engage in mischief (Mailer, *On God* [NY: Random House, 2008]).

because a loving God would not allow such a terrible, final, ultimate evil, He must not exist. As you can see, the atheist concludes what he assumes.

But if God does exist, then death is not the greatest tragedy because it's not the end of our existence but the beginning of a better one. If we have an eternal destiny ahead of us, then the worst fate is not death (which is not bad at all) or suffering (which is temporary) but being stopped in our progress, which is eternal. God will allow us to suffer and die to prevent that fate.

CONCLUSION

The Mormon understanding of God, ourselves, and the purposes of mortality reduces the strength of the argument from evil. While we can all understand and empathize with the doubts that come from experiencing or witnessing intense pain and hardship, the LDS doctrines of the necessity of suffering for growth, the primacy of free will, and the nature of Deity help us see that even this most powerful atheist case against the existence of God is ultimately unpersuasive.

Chapter 2

THE NOT-SO-NEW ATHEISM

A NTIRELIGION ZEALOTS OF THE TWENTY-FIRST century call themselves New Atheists, but there is very little that is new in their arguments. The New Atheism is old atheism recycled and dressed up to fit the latest intellectual fashions. Today's atheists add the word *new* to an old label in order to cash in on our modern society's preoccupation with the "progressive"[1] and cutting edge, but their arguments have been around for more than a century.[2] Marx's atheistic materialism emerged in the mid-nineteenth century. Darwin's *Descent of Man* (not itself atheistic, but giving ammunition to the movement) was published in 1871. Nietzsche wrote his most important works on the death of God and morals in the 1880s. Freud discounted religion as a delusion in

---

1   I use the word "progressive" in quotes because the term is misleading. It implies a political philosophy that assumes 1) history has an inevitable direction, 2) the enlightened know what this direction is, and 3) this direction is good. All three of these propositions are easily refuted by considering 1) the contingency of history, 2) the inability of even the smartest to predict the future, and 3) the many times in history when things have gotten worse. The "conservative" myth, equally mistaken, claims that 1) history has an inevitable direction, 2) the enlightened know what this direction is, and 3) this direction is bad. Ideological myths are poor guides to political thinking and yet, sadly, these two faulty myths dominate our public discourse today.

2   The term "New Atheist" reminds me of BYU philosophy professor Truman Madsen's quip about postmodernism: "There is nothing post or modern about it" (Madsen, personal conversation with the author, August 2004).

the early twentieth century, and logical positivism—which reduces all knowledge to statements about sense data—took off after World War II.

The Book of Mormon anticipated all of the major ideas of these atheists even earlier than that. Two millennia ago, the anti-Christ Korihor (in Alma 30) argued that religion was "the effect of a frenzied mind" (Alma 30:16; an anticipation of Freud) and a tool for the ruling class to "glut [themselves] with the labors" of the workers (Alma 30:27; an anticipation of Marx). He also said that you "cannot know of things which ye do not see" (Alma 30:15; an anticipation of logical positivism), that "every man fared in this life according to the management of the creature" (Alma 30:17; an anticipation of Darwin), and that the end of God meant that "whatsoever a man did was no crime" (Alma 30:17; an anticipation of Nietzsche). The Book of Mormon, published in 1830 and supposedly cooked up by an ignorant farm boy, foresaw the five most important arguments against religion that would define atheism for the coming centuries. Clearly, there is very little that is new about the New Atheism.

ATHEISM IN THE INFORMATION AGE

New Atheist arguments are not only unoriginal; they are also inadequate to the information age in which we now live. From the eighteenth to twentieth centuries, Western nations passed through an industrial era in which machines took over much of humans' physical work. Accordingly, scientists saw the universe itself as a vast machine in which everything could be understood as matter in motion. Even our bodies were machines, and any talk of a soul was, said philosopher Gilbert Ryle, like talking of a "ghost in the machine."[3]

But in our current twenty-first century, post-industrial age, the most crucial component of reality is information—something that is decidedly nonmaterial. The thinking machines (computers) that underlie this new age, while physical, are nothing without the organizing software that makes all of their activity possible. Most of the valuable and real commodities that Americans produce today are not even tangible—including designs, algorithms, soft-copy documents, programs, plans, and spreadsheets. We cannot touch them. They are series of binary code that travel wirelessly

---

3   Gilbert Ryle, *The Concept of Mind* (Chicago: University of Chicago Press, 1949).

through the air and are only discernible on electronic screens. There are billions of machines on the planet (computers) with nonmaterial "ghosts" in them (software). Ryle ridiculed the idea of "ghosts in the machine" while on the very cusp of the new information age in which "ghost-animated" machines would transform the world.

Not only is information more fundamental than matter when it comes to computers, but scientists are now finding that information is even at the root of physics and biology. DNA is an information code that precedes and determines the organization of the matter that makes up living bodies. Atheists claim that humans are mere material beings, but most of the cells of our bodies die and are entirely replaced many times during our lives. Atheists often say, "We don't *have* a body; we *are* a body." If this is true, why do I remain the same while the matter of my body constantly changes? The information coded in our DNA, which determines the structure of our bodies, persists over time. Atheists might not ridicule the idea of a future resurrection if they realized that science itself has shown that this process already happens. The matter comes and goes while the information (the ordering and structuring pattern for the matter) remains.

In physics, quantum theory—developed primarily by Christians such as Max Planck and Werner Heisenberg—has shown that the atomic particles that make up all matter are themselves informational. Electrons exist not as well-defined material entities, but only as probability smears, while the quarks that make up protons and neutrons are so information-laden that some scientists have begun comparing their properties to computer codes.[4] Information is now widely accepted as a third property of the universe along with matter and motion.[5]

While it's common today to use the term *information*, LDS scriptures (prophetic as always) have long called it *intelligence*.[6] In every realm,

---

4   Philip Ball, "We Might Be Living in a Computer Program, But It Might Not Matter," *BBC Earth*, September 5, 2016, accessed January 31, 2016, available at www.bbc.com/earth/story/20160901-we-might-live-in-a-computer-program-but-it-may-not-matter.

5   Stonier T., "Information As a Basic Property of the Universe," *Biosystems*, vol. 38, (1996), 135–40.

6   Early computer scientists, lacking the word *information*, even referred to computer code as intelligence.

ordering intelligence precedes and defines the matter that is ordered. A spiritual creation precedes a physical one (see Moses 3:5), and order presupposes an orderer—a mind that comprehends and creates the order upon which material reality is based. The scriptures refer to both the information that inheres in reality and the mind that understands or creates it as intelligence. This is why we often speak of all matter having intelligence but also refer to God's spirit children as having been created out of eternal intelligences. God, like the humans created in His image, is a creative force—one who can comprehend and create order and information.

While information lies at the foundation of all reality, materialists, who claim the mantle of science, proceed as if science itself hadn't overthrown their view many decades ago. Our postindustrial society is also a post-materialist society, but the New Atheists continue to cling to materialism with as much fervor as any religious fundamentalist clings to the Bible.

INFORMATION IN BIOLOGY

While atheists have not fully come to terms with the information that underlies material reality, they think they can at least get around the problem of order in biology by invoking Darwin's theory of evolution. They claim that the process of natural selection can explain all of those traits that appear to have been designed. The eye, the brain, DNA, for instance, are exceedingly complex biological structures, the atheist concedes, but they can be explained through the survival value they conferred upon humanity's biological ancestors. They don't require a designer, only an unguided Darwinian process— random mutation and natural selection—and a great deal of time.

The most notable proponent of both Darwinism and atheism in the world today is Oxford professor Richard Dawkins. He has gained fame and fortune by advancing the thesis that God is a delusion. Because we can't detect God in empirical, repeatable scientific experiments, Dawkins says, there are no more grounds for believing in God than there are for believing in the Flying Spaghetti Monster. Humans have merely been fooled by evolution into believing in a God who obviously doesn't exist. Once upon a time, says Dawkins, belief in God must have had some survival value—it may have encouraged group solidarity, helped lift the hopeless, or encouraged altruism—but it has now outgrown its usefulness.[7] With today's more advanced scientific viewpoint, he says, we can reject the illusion of God that evolution gave us and live more enlightened, happy lives.

But just because Dawkins and others invoke evolution to justify atheism, this doesn't discredit the theory itself, only the atheists' misuse of it. Evolutionary theory has nothing to say on the materialist question or the existence of God. Although atheists contort a scientific theory to support unrelated conclusions, religious believers should not respond in kind.

Unfortunately, as in so many other realms of life, the debate over evolution has hardened into a dogmatic either/or. Atheists claim that one must choose either evolution or creation, and they accordingly reject creation. Taking the bait, many believers accept that one must choose either evolution or creation and accordingly reject evolution. The simplemindedness of the "evolution versus creation" debate is even played out on car ornaments and bumper stickers.

Latter-day Saints are not stuck with this false choice. Although certain Christians have a doctrinal opposition to the theory of evolution, the LDS Church does not. There is nothing preventing us from believing that God used evolutionary processes to create the diversity of life on our planet.[8] Latter-day prophets have repeatedly reminded us that the Church has no official stance on *how* God created life on earth—that is a matter for the scientists to figure out—only *that* He created life on earth.[9] Some Church leaders have opposed Darwin's theory of evolution (Joseph Fielding Smith and Bruce R. McConkie), while others have accepted it (James E. Talmage, B. H. Roberts, and David O. McKay).[10] God can

7   Dawkins, *The God Delusion*, 200–20.

8   For more on the harmony of evolution and Christianity, see the works of Brown University biologist Kenneth Miller and Human Genome Project director Francis Collins. Both are committed Christians and committed Darwinists.

9   See "What does the Church believe about evolution?," *New Era*, October 2016, accessed January 25, 2016, available at www.lds.org/new-era/2016/10/to-the -point/what-does-the-church-believe-about-evolution?lang=eng.

10   See Joseph Fielding Smith, *Man, His Origin and Destiny* (SLC: Deseret Book, 1954); Bruce R. McConkie, *Mormon Doctrine*, 2nd ed. (SLC: Bookcraft, 1966) 247–56; B. H. Roberts, *The Truth, The Way, and the Life* (Provo, UT: BYU Studies, 1998); Sterling M. McMurrin and L. Jackson Newell, *Matters of Conscience*

create life however He wants, and finding out how He did so is one of the wonders of science.

My own view is that biological evolution, properly understood, harmonizes far better with the gospel than does six-day (or even six-thousand-year) creationism. The scriptures make clear that God did not create life all at once but organized species from existing materials through a long process that began with the simplest organisms and ended with the most complex (man)—exactly as evolutionary theory suggests. Abraham 4:18 even says that God watched the objects of creation "until they obeyed." Joseph Smith spent many sermons hammering home to the Saints the uncomfortable truth that "days" in the scriptures refers to long, indeterminate lengths of time rather than twenty-four-hour periods.[11] Certain Christians reject evolution because it doesn't square with a six-day creation reading of the Bible, but Latter-day Saints are not obligated to adopt this limited view.

Inasmuch as there can be a literal reading of ancient documents, Latter-day Saints do believe in the literal truth of the Bible. That is, we accept its meaning according to the authors' intentions, even as we recognize the meanings they ascribed to words may be different than ours (as the eighth article of faith suggests). For example, when Luke said, "All the world should be taxed" (Luke 2:1), he meant it literally—his whole world was the Roman world with which he was familiar—but he was not using the term *world* as we use it today to refer to the entirety of the planet earth. Or when Matthew mentioned the star over Bethlehem (see Matthew 2:2), he likely meant a bright celestial object and not necessarily a star as modern astronomers use the term (an enormous ball of gas that generates energy through nuclear fusion).

We can, then, read the scriptures literally by accepting the difficulty of translation, understanding ancient peoples on their own terms, and realizing that they operated within different viewpoints, vocabularies,

---

(Salt Lake City: Signature Books, 1996); Gregory A. Prince, *David O. McKay and the Rise of Modern Mormonism* (University of Utah Press: 2005), 45–49; and Carrie Moore, "No Definitive Stance on Evolution, Study Finds," *Deseret News*, March 1, 2006, accessed September 28, 2016, available at www.deseretnews .com/article/635188399/No-definitive-LDS-stance-on-evolution-study-finds .html?pg=all.

11   Joseph Smith made this point on multiple occasions. See, for example, Joseph Smith, "The King Follett Discourse," April 7, 1844, accessed July 3, 2016, available at mldb.byu.edu/follett.htm.

and conceptual frameworks than we do.[12] Joseph Smith taught that "creation" in the Bible meant "organized," and "day" indicated an indefinite time period.[13] The world's definition of "man" has and will continue to change, but Adam was the first man (in the scriptural sense that he was the first to have a relationship with God), the first to have freedom to choose, and the first with a capacity to know good from evil. Since biologists will constantly revise what they mean by "man," it's probably better to stick with the Lord's eternal definitions when reading the scriptures.[14]

Some members might counter that they don't think God would work through evolution, but we might take a cue from Isaiah who taught that God's ways are higher than our ways (see Isaiah 55:8–9). Demanding that God fit *our* narrow, limited notions of how He should operate is, ironically, a central characteristic of the New Atheists themselves.

DESIGN AND EVOLUTION HAND IN HAND

In considering a God who would create through evolution, we must also realize that this is precisely how we humans create. Human artifacts come about through step-by-step micro changes (we might even call them mutations) that are selected for their value. Trial and error decide which changes to retain and which to discard—there is, then, mutation and selection in all human creation.

Ever since the rise of the intelligent design movement in the 1990s, people have regularly placed intelligent design in opposition to evolution,[15] but this is unjustified if we understand that evolution and design work

---

12   The Bible is a work of theology, not science, yet it sometimes seems that too many fundamentalists want to read the scientific parts literally and the theological parts metaphorically.

13   Joseph Smith, "King Follett Discourse."

14   Ironically, many Christian fundamentalists insist on using a twenty-first-century scientific definition of "man," *homo sapien*, when reading Genesis, but then reject that same science when it comes to evolution.

15   See, for instance, Michael Shermer, *Why Darwin Matters: The Case Against Intelligent Design* (NY: Macmillan, 2007); and Ray Comfort, *Intelligent Design vs. Evolution* (Alachua, FL: Bridge Logos Foundation, 2006).

in tandem. Everyone agrees that a computer is the product of intelligent design, yet, as economists Kim Clark (who is now a General Authority) and Carliss Baldwin have shown, it is also the product of Darwinian-type evolution.[16] If humans design through evolution in their creations, couldn't God, who created us in His image, do the same?

Realizing the problem that design in human affairs presents to materialism, some atheists have begun making the argument that design among humans is an illusion. Matt Ridley, for instance, claims that Thomas Edison didn't actually invent the light bulb, phonograph, or kinetoscope—these products simply evolved on their own.[17] Ridley reveals a basic misunderstanding about the nature of invention. Yes, human artifacts come about by evolutionary steps, but human creators are those who *design* the steps. They don't just happen; otherwise we would encourage people across the world in technology, science, business, education, and government to pack up and go home since "evolution will take care of it anyway." Those of us not caught up in materialist thinking realize that, in human affairs, design and evolution work hand in hand. There's no reason this couldn't also be so in the realm of nature and nature's God.

Futurist and *Wired* magazine founder Kevin Kelly has recently pointed out that the whole idea that evolutionary mutations are random is also an unfounded materialist assumption. "The exact nitty-gritty origins of mutations and variations in biology are still uncertain," he says, but "we do know this: variation is emphatically not due to random mutation."[18] All that scientists can say for certain about biological mutations is that they are unpredictable, but unpredictable does not mean unplanned. The evolution of human artifacts is also unpredictable: nobody saw the smartphone coming in the nineteenth century and yet smartphones were decidedly planned by human actors.

Materialists assume that mutations must be random, because if they were not, then where would the nonrandom planning have come from? That, of course, would lead to a designer, and atheists can't let a designer God into the

---

16   See Baldwin and Clark, *Design Rules* (Cambridge, MA: MIT Press, 2000). Clark has previously served as dean of the Harvard Business School and president of BYU–Idaho.

17   Matt Ridley, *The Evolution of Everything* (NY: Harper, 2015).

18   Kevin Kelly, "Postdarwinism," in *Out of Control* (NY: Basic, 1994).

equation. The assumption of randomness in Darwinism is often a product of prejudice, not science, and there is nothing "unscientific" about believing that God planned the mutations that drive evolution forward.

Some scientists have tried to prove that there is no design in biology by creating computer programs that use algorithms to replicate the process of natural selection. This is proof, they say, that there was no design in the emergence of species.

I find this strange: here you have *designers*, *designing* computer programs using *designed* hardware to convince us that *design* is an illusion. They are, of all things, using design to debunk the whole idea of design. Do any of them, I wonder, see the irony? The creators of this evolution replication program design the way that LDS scriptures say that God did: ordering in a conceptual spiritual creation, executing a command, and watching while the creation obeys. Like God, they build creativity into their system. These programmers only prove the point religious believers have long been making: designers are needed to set up the laws and conditions in which evolution unfolds. The mutations in this evolution computer program, then, are hardly random but built into the very nature of the program itself by designers and the rules of selection they created. The New Atheists are wrong: there is nothing inherently atheistic about evolutionary theory.

DARWINIAN FUNDAMENTALISM

My guess is that most Church members don't have a problem with evolution *per se*, but only with an arrogant Darwinian fundamentalism that goes beyond science to claim that evolution is an all-explanatory theory that dispenses with God. While Darwinian *science* claims that evolution explains biodiversity, Darwinian *fundamentalism* claims that evolution explains *everything* (including human consciousness, love, life, religion, morals, decisions, institutions, values, and so forth). Darwinian *science* says evolution is true (inasmuch as scientific theories can be), while Darwinian *fundamentalism* says that evolution is the whole truth and nothing but the truth. Darwinism is a *scientific theory*; Darwinian fundamentalism is a *faith*.

In the Darwinian fundamentalist view, human beings came about purely by chance and are mere animals set apart from their biological relatives only in complexity. There is no essential difference between a human and a monkey or, for that matter, a human and a pile of dirt—all are chance configurations of material. It's the Darwinian fundamentalism of scientists like Richard Dawkins that we should reject, not the theory of evolution itself.

I use the word *fundamentalism* deliberately here. Darwinian fundamentalists do with evolution what some religious fundamentalists do with the Bible: make a single source of truth into a totalizing, all-explanatory paradigm of everything. A Christian fundamentalist might say that all scientific questions can be reduced to religion (found in the Bible), while the Darwinian fundamentalist says that all religious questions can be reduced to science (found in evolution). Many Christian fundamentalists and Darwinian fundamentalists both erroneously believe that evolution—the scientific theory—is the same as Darwinian fundamentalism—the unproven metaphysical (even religious) philosophy.[19]

Sir Karl Popper, the greatest philosopher of science of the twentieth century, helped us understand that scientific theories are those that make falsifiable predictions. If a theory is not open to refutation, then it is not science but religion. By Popper's criterion, Darwinian fundamentalism is a religion, for it can never be disproven through testing (something Popper himself—a great proponent of Darwinism—recognized).[20] Darwinian fundamentalists proclaim that survival (perpetuating our selfish genes) drives all human behavior, yet we humans spend the majority of our time in activities that have no apparent survival value. While it is obvious that eating, earning a livelihood, and attending to our health help us survive, it is not so obvious how attending church, visiting an art gallery, watching television, painting, hanging out with friends, writing poems, going to a service project, Facebooking, playing the piano, or helping a student prepare for an exam would do so. Only creative storytelling and the invocation of unobserved and (ironically) nonmaterial entities called "memes" (Dawkins's name for the cultural equivalent of genes) allow the

---

19   Theologian David Bentley Hart agrees that the New Atheism is fundamentalist at its core, saying, "Atheism that consists entirely in vacuous arguments afloat on oceans of historical ignorance, made turbulent by storms of strident self-righteousness, is as contemptible as any other form of dreary fundamentalism" (Hart, *Atheist Delusions* [New Haven: Yale University Press, 2010], 4).

20   Popper understood that Darwinism at its broadest was not a scientific theory but a useful metaphysical paradigm. See Popper, *The Endless Quest* (Chicago: Open Court, 1982).

Darwinian fundamentalist to universally apply a theory that is so clearly inadequate to explain most of what humans do.

The lack of predictive power in Darwinian fundamentalism is stunning. If we engage in a certain behavior, such as greedily hoarding money, the atheist will say that evolution clearly predicts that behavior because the money can be used to preserve our lives and that of our offspring (buying food, shelter, or health care, for instance). But notice that if we engage in the *exact opposite behavior* by sharing money with a stranger, the atheist will claim evolution predicts that behavior too because we can hope that the stranger will return the favor and thereby (via what biologists call reciprocal altruism) enhance our survival as well.

Given such creative storytelling, what could ever falsify the idea that Darwinism explains everything? How would the scientific community have received Einstein if he predicted that light would both bend and not bend when crossing the path of a star? Don't atheists laugh at astrologers who predict everything such that their predictions are never wrong? Don't they scoff when religious believers take both blessings and trials as evidence of God's power? How is it any different when they, in their Darwinian fundamentalism, predict opposites and take everything as a sign of evolution's power? Any theory that predicts one thing and the opposite thing at the same time is unfalsifiable and therefore nonscientific—it's a matter of faith. Evolutionary biologist Austin Hughes noted the following:

> Biologists as well as philosophers have all too often been guilty of . . . storytelling rather than hypothesis-testing in the scientific sense. For a complete evolutionary account of a phenomenon, it is not enough to construct a story about how the trait might have evolved in response to a given selection pressure; rather, one must provide some sort of evidence that it really *did* so evolve. This is a very tall order, especially when we are dealing with human mental or behavioral traits, the genetic basis of which we are far from understanding.[21]

Even convinced atheists are starting to point out the obvious flaws and circular reasoning of Darwinian fundamentalism. Jerry Fodor and Massimo Piattelli-Palmarini argue that much of what we consider Darwinian science these days is actually making up "just so stories" to

---

21   Austin L. Hughes, "The Folly of Scientism," *The New Atlantis*, Fall 2012, accessed July 13, 2016, available at www.thenewatlantis.com/publications/the-folly-of -scientism; italics in original.

expand Darwinism's explanatory capabilities beyond the evidence.[22] Renowned psychologist Amos Tversky, becoming frustrated with the unscientific storytelling of evolutionary psychology, said, "Listen to evolutionary psychologists long enough, and you'll stop believing in evolution."[23] And Harvard geneticist Richard Lewontin pointed out that "the telling of a plausible evolutionary story without any possibility of critical and empirical verification has become an accepted mode of intellectual work even in natural science. . . . Biologists are always able to provide plausible scenarios for evolution by natural selection. But plausibility is not science."[24]

Even these atheists understand that Darwinism has its place, but if we elevate it into an all-encompassing theory of *everything*, we are going beyond science and into the realm of religion.

We might understand Darwinian fundamentalism a bit better by comparing it to Marxism. There is plenty of evidence to confirm Marx's central insight that economic interests and class relations motivate human behavior. For instance, we can usually predict American presidential elections by looking at the country's economic performance under the incumbent party. But Marx made the error of using this insight to explain *every* human activity. This led Marx and his followers to see religion, art, commerce, creativity, war, political rule, police actions, associations, technology, entrepreneurship, and education in terms of class. Worse yet, his followers applied the theory to governance and created some of the most oppressive tyrannies in world history. The problem with Marxists is not their theory but that they transformed a useful theory from *one* way to look at things into the *only* way to look at things.[25]

---

22 Jerry Fodor and Massimo Piattelli-Palmarini, *What Darwin Got Wrong* (NY: Farrar, Straus, and Giroux, 2010).

23 Cass Sunstein and Richard Thaler, "The Two Friends Who Changed How We Think About How We Think," *The New Yorker*, December 7, 2016, accessed January 27, 2017, available at www.newyorker.com/books/page-turner/the-two -friends-who-changed-how-we-think-about-how-we-think.

24 Richard Lewontin, "Not So Natural Selection," *New York Review of Books*, May 27, 2010.

25 Conversely, we might also compare Darwinism to the economic theory of Adam Smith. Despite its remarkable ability to predict human behavior and guide us in

Atheists are guilty of the same with Darwinian fundamentalism. Asking people to believe in the totalizing powers of Marxism or Darwinism is asking them to take a leap of faith that a scientific approach to reality should forbid. The best scholarship would accept the useful in Darwin and Marx while also recognizing the limitations inherent in both.

While we want to be ecumenical and work with our brothers and sisters of other Christian denominations, this does not entail tethering ourselves to the flaws in their theology. One of the great strengths of LDS doctrine is how well it squares with science, including the findings of biology. To turn away from this strength in order to better align with certain strands of fundamentalist Christianity would be a mistake.

ATHEISM AND FINE-TUNING

Although evolution does not refute the case for design in biology, recent findings in cosmology show that evidence for design in the universe is stronger than ever. Scientists are realizing more every day that the universe is perfectly set up for our species to come into being. That is, if any one of the thousands of the physical constants of the universe were the slightest bit different, then human life never would have emerged.[26] The probability that every single physical constant would have had exactly these values is essentially zero—it's an impossibility. "The more I examine the universe and the details of its architecture, the more evidence I find that the universe in some sense must have known we were coming," said physicist Freeman Dyson.[27] Theologians call this the "argument from fine-tuning" while scientists call it the "anthropic principle." In the face of

---

setting up institutions to generate economic growth, Smith's classical economic theory is not all-explanatory. There are the problems of human irrationality, imperfect information, externalities, and so forth that require correction within a market framework. Certain dogmatic economists deny any problems with Smith's ideas, but they are changing the facts to fit the theory instead of vice versa. We find the same tendency among Darwinian fundamentalists that we find among economic fundamentalists.

26   Science writer and humorist Bill Bryson makes this point eloquently in the first chapter of his bestselling book, *A Short History of Nearly Everything* (NY: Broadway Books, 2003).

27   Dyson, *Disturbing the Universe* (NY: Basic Books, 1979), 250.

this evidence for design, physicist Fred Hoyle was led to doubt his athe-ism, saying, "the universe looks like a put-up job," and crusading atheist Antony Flew completely changed his mind and turned to belief in God.[28]

Hardened atheists, though, are not persuaded by the argument from fine-tuning. Matt Ridley says it is no more miraculous that life just happens to fit the conditions of the universe than it is that rainwater just happens to fit the shape of a pothole—life naturally emerged to suit the given parame-ters.[29] But what Ridley doesn't realize is that the miracle is in the parameters themselves. It's as if the pothole was shaped to spell out the phrase, "Hello, Matt Ridley," giving clear evidence of design in the shape of the pothole rather than in the rainwater that fits it. The miracle is not that any universe exists with things adapting to fit that universe, but that a specific kind of universe exists that would bring forth the wonders of human life and experience.

Other atheists bypass a designer God by positing the existence of an infinite number of universes, at least one of which would eventually pro-duce human life.[30] This view is most associated with the famous physicist Stephen Hawking, who hypothesized that black holes could create "baby universes." If each universe begins in a singularity—an infinitely mas-sive and infinitely dense point in space-time—then more singularities (black holes) might mean more universes and, given enough universes, something like human life would inevitably emerge.[31]

Of course, there is no empirical evidence for the existence of these alter-native universes, but Hawking and other atheists assume they exist because it is their only defense against the overwhelming evidence for cosmic design. Bringing imagined, unseen entities in to support a theory seems a strange

---

28   See Antony Flew, *There Is a God: How the World's Most Notorious Atheist Changed His Mind* (NY: HarperCollins, 2008).

29   Ridley, *The Evolution of Everything*.

30   For more on the multiverse hypothesis, see Max Tegmark, "Parallel Universes," *Scientific American*, May 2003; and Stephen Hawking and Leonard Mlodinow, *The Grand Design* (NY: Bantam, 2010).

31   See Hawking, *Black Holes and Baby Universes and Other Essays* (NY: Bantam, 1993).

thing for committed empiricists to do.[32] They reject God on the grounds that we can't see Him, but then accept the existence of infinite universes even though we can't see those either. As physicist Paul Davies said in a *New York Times* opinion piece, "Invoking an infinity of unseen universes to explain the unusual features of the one we do see is just as *ad hoc* as invoking an unseen Creator. The multiverse theory may be dressed up in scientific language, but in essence it requires the same leap of faith."[33] Perhaps atheists are not so committed to science but only to the idea of a godless universe in which they have no religious obligations.

Ironically, the "multiverse hypothesis" makes the existence of God more, not less, likely since atheists then not only have to confront the question "Does God exist?" but also "Will God exist?" If, as atheists suggest, an infinite number of universes would inevitably do one impossible thing—generate human life—then an infinite number of universes would also inevitably do another impossible thing—generate God. If we exist, with our capacities to create wonders such as computers, spaceships, clones, modern medicine, blockbuster movies, scientific theories, and literature, and all of this came about by pure chance, then it is only a matter of time until that same pure chance produces a being who can create life, construct earths, conquer mortality, forgive sins, and help other beings in the cosmos advance to become like Him. To say that infinite universes will inevitably produce something as unlikely as rational human beings means that infinite universes will also inevitably produce something as unlikely as an omniscient, omnipotent, everlasting being that has the attributes we Latter-day Saints ascribe to God.

Either God exists because He fine-tuned this universe for human habitation, or He exists because there was an infinite number of multiverses of which He was an inevitable by-product. Either way, He exists.[34]

---

32 According to Freeman Dyson, "The multiverse is philosophy and not science. Science is about facts that can be tested and mysteries that can be explored, and I see no way of testing hypotheses of the multiverse" (Dyson, "What Can You Really Know?" *New York Review of Books*, November 8, 2012).

33 Paul Davies, "A Brief History of the Multiverse," *New York Times*, April 12, 2003, accessed July 14, 2016, available at www.nytimes.com/2003/04/12/opinion/a -brief-history-of-the-multiverse.html?pagewanted=all.

34 Truman Madsen independently came to this same conclusion. See his audio lecture series, *Timeless Questions, Gospel Insights*, available from Deseret Book.

In turning to the multiverse hypothesis to avoid the fine-tuning problem, atheists have circled right back to the God they ran away from in
the first place.

ARGUMENT FROM PRESERVATION

If our existence weren't miraculous enough, our *continued* existence is yet another miracle that requires explaining. Not only is it a
sign of Providence that we are here, but it is also a sign of Providence
that we remain here from moment to moment. Life brought into existence by completely random means could at any time be destroyed by
equally random means (a meteorite, natural disaster, famine, plague,
or climate change). What makes our existence so resilient? A virus
could mutate and wipe out all humans just as easily as it kills a few of
us. Why doesn't it? Some atheists would say (assuming the foresight
among biological organisms that is supposed to be forbidden among
Darwinian fundamentalists) that it is not in the interest of a patho-
gen to kill its host, but if that were so, then why did the Black Death
and myriad other plagues do exactly that? And if such diseases could
kill nearly 50 percent of the population of Europe, then why not 100
percent of the population of Earth? Random mutations are random,
after all, and, under materialism, there's no reason a virus couldn't
mutate to kill every human life on the planet.

Some atheists dismiss the argument from fine-tuning, saying that our
existence isn't mysterious or miraculous because if things hadn't turned
out this way, we wouldn't be around to talk about it. But, as philosopher
John Leslie has pointed out, that's like saying it's not improbable that a
condemned criminal was hit by none of the dozens of bullets shot by a
firing squad simply because the criminal remained around to talk about
it. Leslie doesn't go far enough, though, because the bullets continue
flying at every second and yet we continue to exist.

Matt Ridley is an atheist, but his book *The Rational Optimist* makes
an implicit case for God in showing that humans have been up against
the brink of destruction dozens of times, yet have miraculously developed
a way out each time (for example, an agricultural productivity revolution right at the moment when Malthusian population explosions should

have killed most of us).[35] Ridley chronicles miracle after miracle but he doesn't even see them for what they are. He ridicules the idea of design in the universe, yet all of the perfect coincidences necessary for humans to have survived their own history make the case that there is a sustaining designer coming through for us time and again.[36] A higher power ensures not just that we are here but that we remain here.

The evidence for design in the universe shouldn't surprise Latter-day Saints since it is one of the few arguments for God's existence found in the Book of Mormon. Alma 30:44 says, "All things denote there is a God; yea, even the earth, and all things that are upon the face of it, yea, and its motion, yea, and also all the planets which move in their regular form do witness that there is a Supreme Creator."

In his own language, Alma was observing the fine tuning that is visible all around us and noting that the order of the cosmos requires an orderer—God.

CONCLUSION

Not only is little new in the New Atheism, but this view is also becoming more antiquated every day as we move further toward a world in which design, intelligence, information, and order are recognized as fundamental to reality. Atheistic materialism is an obsolete vestige of the nineteenth-century industrial outlook, so it's time that believers and unbelievers alike faced up to the fact that the New Atheism is a misnomer.

---

35   Ridley, *The Rational Optimist* (NY: HarperCollins, 2010).

36   This could be because of either direct divine intervention or God's foreknowledge, but the distinction is irrelevant here.

Chapter 3

ATHEISM AND MIND

WE LIVE IN A SPIRITUAL world the same way a fish lives in water. Since our very minds are nonmaterial, things of a spiritual nature surround us, permeate our experience, and form the backdrop of everything we do. It is mind through which we read these words. It is mind through which we comprehend them. It is mind through which we form images and words of our own. It is mind through which we evaluate something as good or evil, true or false. It is mind through which we chose to pick up this book (when our instincts were telling us to do something less taxing, like watch reruns of *Seinfeld*). This consciousness, this awareness, this imagination, this selfhood, this unique capacity to think, conceptualize, order, know, evaluate, and choose can all fall under the general heading "mind."

In the scriptures, the word *intelligence* appears to be used as a synonym for *mind* (D&C 93:29–31; Abraham 3:21–23). Intelligence, with the knowing, choosing, and creating it entails, is unique to humans and fundamental to our existence. Monkeys, for all of the material characteristics they share with us, only follow DNA programming. Computers, for all of their sophistication and calculating power, still only follow software programming. In having mind, humans are, with God, in a class of their own.

To emphasize human kinship with animals, atheists often point out that we share 98 percent of our DNA with chimpanzees,[1] but this figure actually weakens their case since it shows how very little the material part

---

1 A number of self-published books indicate that this is a widespread view among common atheists. See, for instance, Geoff Linsley, *The Atheist's Bible: How Science Eliminates Theism* (Bloomington, IN: iUniverse, Inc., 2008), 189; and Brett Stillman, *The Confessions of a Moral Atheist* (Bloomington, IN: Xlibris Corporation, 2006), 99–101.

of us counts. If we share 98 percent of our material with chimps, then why are we infinitely different? Can chimps make 98 percent of a skyscraper, write 98 percent of a book, create 98 percent of our economic output, or produce 98 percent of a computer? The "98 percent chimp DNA" figure only emphasizes the insignificance of matter and the importance of that "something else" about humans—mind—that transcends the material.

Mind is even more fundamental and undeniable for people than water is for a fish, yet we often take this spiritual side of reality for granted. Only the pervasiveness of water would allow the fish to question the existence of water, and only the pervasiveness of spirit allows the atheist to question the existence of spirit.

HOW ATHEISTS DENY MIND

Because the existence of mind would falsify the materialist paradigm, atheists are desperate to deny its reality. They attempt to do so by invoking reductionism, which says that all characteristics we associate with mind can be reduced to brain function. Mind, in other words, has no independent reality; it is produced by the brain.[2]

This attempt to reduce mind to brain has thus far been based mostly on wishful thinking. Neurosurgeon Eben Alexander points out that "science can't even provide the first sentence for explaining consciousness," and even most convinced atheists admit that there is a "hard problem of consciousness."[3] Ed Witten, a leading mathematical physicist, even concluded that, regardless of our advances in brain science, "consciousness will remain a mystery."[4] Mind is fundamentally different than matter,

---

2   Dennett, *Consciousness Explained* (Boston: Back Bay Books, 1992); and Harris, *The End of Faith*, chapter 7.

3   Eben Alexander, "Death is Not Final," Intelligence Squared Debate, May 7, 2014. The most introspective popular philosopher of the twentieth century, Jean Paul Sartre emphasized the importance of consciousness but concluded it was ultimately the "nothingness" at the heart of being. Sartre, *Being and Nothingness* (London: Methuen, 1956). But to dismiss the most important element of being itself simply by declaring it "nothingness" is not an adequate way to proceed.

4   See interview with Ed Witten at The Curious Wave Function website, accessed August 27, 2016, available at wavefunction.fieldofscience.com/2016/08/physicist -ed-witten-on-consciousness-i.html?m=1.

but as a materialist article of faith, atheists continue to insist that mind must be a by-product of the material brain.

There is no known path by which mind can come from matter. There never could be. It's not that science has yet to find an explanation for consciousness (it hasn't) but that it can't. Consciousness is decidedly invisible and nonmaterial, so it falls outside the domain of scientific explanation. How to get nonmaterial (consciousness) from material (a brain) is a question no scientist could conceivably answer, and their attempts to do so lead them into untestable, unscientific speculation. The very act of thinking reveals this to the conscious self. Getting mind from meat, according to journalist David Brooks, is simply impossible.[5]

The brain's relationship to consciousness is similar to the eye's relationship to sight. It is through the eyeball that the brain receives the data that becomes sight, but sight is not the eyeball. Sight is perception of images of the world in all its wonder; the eyeball is a chunk of interconnected tissues. Eyes are merely a tool through which our sight is filtered, and brains are merely a tool through which our minds are filtered. Damage to the eye can cause reduction in sight as damage to the brain can cause reduction in thought, but that doesn't change the reality that eye is not sight and brain is not mind.

French philosopher René Descartes established the reality of mind centuries ago in his *Meditations,* noting that he could doubt everything, even his perceptions, but not the fact that he was doubting. The reality of his conscious thinking was the only thing he was absolutely certain of. "I think, therefore I am." Other philosophers have made the same point in a more commonsense way by responding to the question, "How do I know I exist?" with, "Who is speaking?"[6] And when we say, "I exist," we are not saying that a certain arrangement of atoms exists but that a thinking self—a nonmaterial mind—exists.

Atheists since Descartes, despite their considerable efforts, have not been able to overcome the commonsense, irrefutable, and utterly miraculous fact that "I exist." But they keep trying. They argue that correlation between mental functioning and brain physiology is evidence that brain causes mind. For instance, Bruce Hood says that "we know the self is

5   David Brooks, "Beyond the Brain," *New York Times,* June 17, 2013.

6   Alan Greenspan, *The Age of Turbulence* (NY: Penguin, 2008), 41.

constructed because it can be so easily deconstructed through damage [to the brain],"[7] yet a basic principle of science is that correlation is not causation. Somehow materialist neuroscientists assume that just because a brain state is *correlated* with a mental experience, the brain state must be *causing* the experience. This is as unwarranted as saying emergency rooms cause deaths because deaths correlate with visits to the emergency room or that a television set creates shows because the availability of shows correlates with the TV being on.[8] A television set can be damaged and thereby transmit a show less perfectly (or not at all), but that hardly means the television set *is* the show (or produces the show). And yet, using the same logic, atheists continue to assert that the brain *is* the mind (or produces the mind).

Psychologist Susan Blackmore makes a similar error, saying, "Consciousness is not some weird and wonderful product of some brain processes, but not others. Rather, it's an illusion constructed by a clever brain and body in a complex social world."[9] This is tantamount to saying that you know books are an illusion because you read it in a book or that the Internet is an illusion because a Web page told you so. All of the scientific data about brain imaging that Blackmore used to come to this conclusion came *through* her consciousness. All of the evidence she uses to deny consciousness itself *depends* upon consciousness.

In fact, as Descartes's reasoning makes clear, consciousness is far more certain than the data Blackmore relies on to dismiss consciousness. She may have been dreaming that she saw the brain scans, but she could not have been dreaming that she was conscious when she saw them because even dreams and hallucinations are conscious experiences. Nonetheless,

---

7   Bruce Hood, "The Self," in *This Idea Must Die*, 147. Later in the essay he makes another logical mistake saying, "The self is an illusion because it feels so real." By this reasoning, those things that seem least real, like leprechauns, wizards, and dragons, must be the most real and those things that seem most real, like my house, family, and colleagues, must be illusory.

8   In denying mind, materialists are also caught in circular reasoning. Since material is all there is, then they assume there must be a material explanation for mind, so they invent material explanations for mind to match their assumption which, in turn, leads them to conclude that material is all there is.

9   Susan Blackmore, "The Neural Correlates of Consciousness," in *This Idea Must Die*, 143.

the materialist dogma tells her, *a priori* (before the fact), that consciousness must be an illusion. It simply has to be since it can't square with materialism.

Atheists say that extraordinary claims require extraordinary evidence. I can think of no more extraordinary claim than "consciousness is an illusion," but instead of providing extraordinary evidence for this claim, atheists provide none at all.

Philosopher John Searle has attempted to demystify mind by applying the term *emergent property* to it. Just as wetness emerges as a unique property from hydrogen and oxygen molecules, says Searle, so mind emerges as a unique property from the brain. As cosmologist David Christian explains, "I and all the complex things around me . . . don't exist 'in' the bits and pieces that made them; they emerge from the arrangement of those bits and pieces in very precise ways. And that is also true of the emergent entities known as 'you' and 'me'."[10]

Applying the term *emergent* to mind or the self does nothing to explain it but only gives it a label. Giving a scientific-sounding name to something that is inherently nonscientific does not solve the problem. Mind remains a mystery that Searle can't simply dismiss by appealing to neologism or analogy.

Literary theorists try to get rid of mind by claiming that the self is a linguistic construct that can be exposed through deconstruction. All conceptions of reality, they claim, are creations of language, and inasmuch as humans are embedded in linguistic webs of meaning, our very notions of self and individuality are also products of that language.[11] We can reject Descartes's claim, "I think, therefore I am," because it was expressed in language—the language creates the self, not vice versa.

This argument fails to realize that although language might influence our perceptions of reality, this does not mean that it *changes* reality. Just because our conception of snow is affected by our words used to describe snow (Eskimos famously have many more words for snow than we do), this does nothing to change the reality of snow itself. Although people of different cultural-linguistic frameworks may use different words to

---

10   David Christian, "The Idea of Emergence," in John Brockman, ed., *This Explains Everything* (NY: Harper Perennial, 2013), 176.

11   Jacques Derrida, *Of Grammatology* (Baltimore: Johns Hopkins University Press, 1974); Michel Foucault, *The Order of Things* (NY: Routledge, 2001), 422.

describe mind, this has no effect on the reality of mind.[12] Many scientists have dubbed literary deconstruction "fashionable nonsense," and even Richard Dawkins is rightfully dismissive of its most outlandish claims.[13]

There is also no direct evidence that language creates consciousness or the self. Atheists have never observed it happen. It is an untestable speculation they employ because they have nowhere else to turn to explain this amazing thing we call mind. Atheists will believe extremely complex and unlikely ideas (in contravention of Occam's razor) to avoid the obvious truth that mind has an independent reality.

The most obvious way to test the proposition that language creates consciousness would be to examine a nonlinguistic person. But without a linguistic interface we would have no way to ask or receive an answer to the question, "Are you conscious?" Perhaps the best we can do, then, is to look at cases of people both blind and deaf who grew up without language but then developed it later in life and had memory of their prelinguistic state. Helen Keller fits the bill, and her autobiography suggests that she had mind, consciousness, and awareness long before she had language. Her very ability to remember the moment she acquired language at a water pump (and the frustrations of her life before that point) deal a severe blow to the "language produces consciousness" view.[14]

Deconstructionist attempts to get rid of mind also fall into the trap of preferring the uncertain to the certain. They try to explain away the undeniable knowledge we have of our own existence by appealing to highly speculative, untested ideas floating around in academic circles. Deconstruction is based on hypothetical and tenuous linguistic theories, but

---

12 Linguistic constructivism has been seriously weakened by recent studies that suggest that core concepts are inborn and hardwired into the brain, not learned. This theory of a universal grammar was the great contribution of linguist Noam Chomsky, who has since become one of the most well-known intellectual critics of American foreign policy.

13 Dawkins, "Postmodernism Disrobed," 141–43.

14 Helen Keller, *The Story of My Life* (NY: Grosset and Dunlap, 1905), 9–24. The fact that children have concepts before they have the language to express those concepts also appears to falsify the linguistic constructivist view. For instance, my one-year-old son grasped the category of photograph before he knew the word *photograph* (and used the word we had applied to the content of a picture to describe all photographs until we taught him otherwise).

since we are all infinitely more convinced of our own existence than we are of the validity of those theories, why throw out certainties in favor of uncertainties?

Other materialists, confronted with the hard problem of consciousness, try to explain away mind using the computer as an analogy. The self or mind, they say, is simply a by-product of complex neural circuitry, and someday computers—with enough processing power and memory—will be as conscious as humans. We will know when computers have reached this consciousness using the Turing test. Once a hidden computer is able to fool us by its language alone into thinking that it is a human being, it will at that point be as conscious as the rest of us.

Atheists here make the fundamental error of confusing "fooling" and "being." Fooling someone into thinking that A is B does not actually make A into B. For instance, I can don a costume and fool people into thinking I'm a gorilla; that hardly makes me an actual gorilla. If I use white paint and disguise a rock as a marshmallow, I am not making it puffy and sugary—it is still a rock. And if a computer passes the Turing test by fooling people into thinking it is conscious, it hasn't actually become conscious. Thus, the Turing test fails when it comes to determining the reality of mind.

The aforementioned atheist philosopher John Searle actually provided a refutation of the idea that computers can develop minds with his "Chinese room" thought experiment. Imagine, said Searle, an American who speaks no Chinese enclosed in a room with a book that instructs him how to respond to patterns of Chinese characters. Each time someone passes tablets with Chinese characters through a slit in the wall, this American could go to the instruction book and, based on what it said, slide tablets back that contained intelligible Chinese information. The person inside the room would have no understanding of the Chinese characters but would have the appearance of understanding simply by following instructions. That's what a computer does, says Searle. There is no consciousness or awareness at work, only the executing of commands. The computer processes information but never comprehends, grasps, knows, chooses, or imagines. Consciousness and computing are fundamentally different things, and since computational power is not mind, increasing computational power cannot get us any closer to mind.[15]

---

15 John Searle, "The Chinese Room," in R. A. Wilson and F. Keil, eds., *The MIT Encyclopedia of the Cognitive Sciences* (Cambridge: MIT Press, 1999).

David Gelernter, a professor of computer science at Yale, points out that the very comparison between minds and computers is misguided. A computer is a series of on/off switches. So is a network of train tracks, yet we would hardly say that this makes train tracks conscious. Yes, computers, like minds, can perform calculations, says Gelernter, but that is only one of the infinite functions that minds perform. Minds, unlike computers, can feel pain, be offended, change perspectives, reflect on actions, adopt new paradigms, choose alternatives, determine value, self-correct, and so forth. When minds and computers are so radically different, says Gelernter, the idea that computers could ever become minds is as preposterous as saying train tracks could become minds.[16]

We might also refute the "mind as computer" argument by considering the unitary nature of consciousness. There has been some talk lately about the possibility of uploading one's brain to a computer. By copying a person's neural patterns onto a complex machine, this theory states that a person could cheat death and live on indefinitely with their "self" existing in a computer. If mind were equal to brain, this might be possible.

But what would happen to "you" once your brain was uploaded? If you copied your own neural patterns to a computer would "you" then be whipped out of your body and into the computer, leaving your body a zombie? If not, then the self or mind would remain in the body even if the brain wiring were duplicated. "You" wouldn't be on the computer—only a neurological pattern would—meaning that you are distinct from that neurological pattern and the mind is not the brain.

And if "I" could be uploaded to a computer, then "I" could also be uploaded to two (or more) computers, meaning that "I" (a singular entity) would then become an "us" (a plural entity) at the same time—a logical impossibility.[17] Material is divisible—I can always cut up matter into

---

16 David Gelernter, *The Tides of Mind: Uncovering the Spectrum of Consciousness*. (NY: W. W. Norton, 2016); and David Gelernter interview with Russ Roberts, *EconTalk* podcast, November 7, 2016, accessed November 10, 2016, available at www.econtalk.org/archives/2016/11/david_gelernter.html.

17 Some might argue that Multiple Personality Disorder (MPD) shows that consciousness can, indeed, be plural, but consciousness is different than personality. Those with MPD do not experience multiple consciousness; rather, they experience a single consciousness that appears to switch back and forth between different personalities. MPD is one consciousness manifesting multiple personalities, not multiple consciousness manifesting multiple personalities.

smaller pieces—but consciousness is indivisible, ergo consciousness can't be material. This "dual mind" problem seems to me a convincing disproof of materialism.

We must conclude that mind is independent of matter, and if it is, then there is no reason to believe it won't continue to exist once the matter associated with it (the brain) is dead. We don't need computers to give us immortality; the immaterial mind is itself sufficient for that.

Atheists, not believing in life after death, though, claim that when we die we go from consciousness to oblivion. That seems somewhat plausible until we realize this implies the reverse: we once went from oblivion to consciousness. That's almost as difficult an idea to accept. It is, literally, a miracle. Atheists who claim that it's supernatural nonsense to believe that the mind survives the death of the body are stuck with a reality at least as strange: that mind emerged from nothing. That's just as supernatural. Atheists often demand that believers show them "miracles," but the reality of mind itself is a miracle available for all to experience.

C. S. Lewis, during the grief following his wife's death, realized that either she still existed or she had never existed in the first place. That is, the "she" that he loved was not something material. He didn't love the cells, the hair, the fingernails, the joints, the bones, or the muscles; he loved "her"—something independent of and irreducible to the physical components of his wife's body.[18] *We* exist, and *we* are not material.

Atheist materialism is ultimately just the latest in a long line of failed attempts to establish philosophical monism—the idea that all of reality is just one substance. Pre-Socratic Greek philosophers such as Thales, Anaximenes, and Anaximander variously put forward water, air, or apeiron as the one true reality, but monism works no better today than it did in ancient Greece. It's obvious that there is a material reality, but it's equally obvious that there is a mental reality. The prophet Lehi taught that there is a basic duality of being—things to act (mind) and things to be acted upon (matter) (see 2 Nephi 2:14). Mind is real, matter is real, and mind is not matter. These realms are irreducibly distinct, and no amount of modern sophistry can get beyond this fact. All philosophies that deny this plain truth by trying to reduce matter to mind or vice versa become caught in absurdity. This means that atheistic materialism, according to the most basic intuitions we have, is manifestly false.

---

18   C. S. Lewis, *A Grief Observed* (NY: HarperOne, 2009).

SCIENCE AND MIND

Recent scientific discoveries are only strengthening the case for the independent reality of mind. According to quantum mechanics, matter actually changes in response to mental events. Human observation of sub-atomic particles *alters the behavior of those particles.* Heisenberg's uncertainty principle rests on the idea that the position and velocity of electrons or photons are indeterminate until they are consciously observed. Not only can mind change the behavior of matter nearby, but it can alter the behavior of twin particles light years away. In one experiment at Princeton University, people were even able to alter random number generation from a distance simply by concentrating their minds on a particular number.[19]

The reality of neuroplasticity also defies materialist reasoning. Research is showing that humans can rewire their own brains through acts of will.[20] Mind, it's now clear, can change even the most fundamental facts of our biology. Mind is not a function of matter; mind can determine and control matter.

The placebo effect defeats the case for materialism as well. Patients who take false medicines still find themselves improving in health, simply because of the change in their mental state. If materialism were true, how is it that a nonmaterial mental event (belief in a false medicine) could have effects on material (the body)? The material conditions for a patient haven't changed; only the mental conditions have. "Mind over matter" is no longer just a nice slogan. It is a scientific fact.[21]

The mind over matter principle also helps illuminate the nature of creation. God, through an act of will, shapes matter and controls the universe

19   See Robert Lanza with Bob Berman, *Biocentrism: How Life and Consciousness are the Keys to Understanding the True Nature of the Universe* (Dallas: Benbella Books, 2009); and The Global Consciousness Project, accessed July 31, 2016, information available at noosphere.princeton.edu. For an overview of the findings, see: noosphere.princeton.edu/introduction.html.

20   See, for example, Moheb Costandi, *Neuroplasticity* (Cambridge: MIT Press, 2016); and Carol Dweck, *Mindset* (NY: Ballantine, 2007).

21   Dogmatic materialists, confronted with this reality, must get very creative to argue their way out. They claim that one set of brain parameters (the illusion of the will) is affecting another set of brain parameters (the changed brain wiring). Again, they try to get around the problem simply by rephrasing it. They are merely pretending to have a solution when all they really have are words.

instead of letting it control Him. He, like us, is a being to act rather than be acted upon—a cause rather than an effect. Will not only transcends the material world but manipulates, organizes, and masters it. Contrary to the atheist assertions that mind is matter, it turns out that mind triumphs *over* matter and has measurable effects on the physical world.[22]

FREE WILL

Bound up with the reality of mind is freedom of the will. Although atheists assure us that we humans are mere material, we constantly do a very unmaterial thing: make choices. Unlike matter, which simply follows the causal laws of physics, and unlike other animals, who are bound by instincts, human beings can choose their actions. We can refuse to eat when hungry (fast), refuse to engage in vengeance when angry (forgive), refuse intoxicating substances when enticed (temperance), and so forth.

Free will holds a special place in LDS theology. For Mormons, agency is not simply the nice ability to make choices but entails the power to progress and become more like God. Our destiny and ultimate goal—eternal life—is bound up with agency. Intelligence, and the associated capacity to choose at the core of our being, is self-existent and uncreated (see D&C 93; Abraham 3). It's the primal stuff from which God fashioned our spirits.

Other great thinkers have recognized the centrality of conscious choice to existence. German philosopher Edmund Husserl taught that we should make consciousness the central object of philosophical inquiry. By bracketing out all objects of thought and focusing internally on consciousness itself, we find that "intentionality" (and the imagination and free choice it entails) is the defining characteristic of human beings. Even though Husserl, a Christian, had many atheist disciples in the "existentialist" tradition (most notably John Paul Sartre), they nonetheless recognized intentionality and choice as the fundamental characteristics that separated human existence (*Dasein* in Heidegger's terminology) from all else that is.[23] In the words of neuroscientist Mario Beauregard, "We are not

---

22   See, for instance, Lanza and Berman, *Biocentrism*.

23   For more on Husserl's philosophy see Edmund Husserl, *The Logical Investigations*, 2 vols. (1901, 1902); and Dallas Willard, *Logic and the Objectivity of Knowledge* (Athens, OH: Ohio University Press, 1984).

biological robots totally governed by "selfish" genes and neurons. . . . We can intentionally create new social and cultural environments. Through us, evolution becomes conscious, that is, it is driven not simply by drives for survival and reproduction but more by complex sets of insights, goals, desires, and beliefs."[24]

Latter-day Saints have a related view. We believe that our intentional thoughts make us part of Lehi's category of "things to act" rather than "things to be acted upon." The reaching, choosing, creative, proactive nature of consciousness is what makes us children of God.

Since our eternal progress is predicated upon the exercise of agency, it makes sense that Lucifer would have tried to restrict it in the pre-earth life, and it makes sense that atheists would wish to deny its reality today. Most atheists reject the reality of free will, claiming that it, like mind, is an illusion.[25] Biologist Jerry Coyne even declared that the very idea of agency should die. Materialism, he says, "puts paid to the traditional idea of a dualistic or 'libertarian' free will: that our lives comprise a series of decisions in which we could have chosen otherwise. We know now that we can never do otherwise. 'I'—whatever 'I' means—may have the illusion of choosing, but my choices are in principle predictable by the laws of physics. In short, the traditional notion of free will . . . is dead on arrival."[26]

Coyne's position is actually refuted by numerous recent studies that suggest that the denial of agency is self-fulfilling: the more you deny your agency, the less ability you *actually have* to exercise it. For instance, experiments have shown that people are more likely to cheat on a test after reading an argument against free will. Researchers have also found that as a belief in free will has declined among undergraduates, honesty has declined as well. As they learn from their professors that they are "mere materials" being controlled by their genetics and environment, they then engage in dishonest behaviors under the belief that "they couldn't have done otherwise." Surveys have shown that the higher people score on their belief in free will, the more control they actually have over their lives, the

---

24   Beauregard, *The Spiritual Brain*, 152.

25   See, for instance, the essays of Thomas Metzinger, Susan Blackmore, Bruce Hood, and Jerry Coyne in *This Idea Must Die*.

26   Coyne, "Free Will," in *This Idea Must Die*, 154.

better they do in their jobs, and the more life satisfaction they enjoy.[27] The mindset you cultivate, according to psychologist Carol Dweck, determines how much impact your will actually has over your life. If you think you are a slave to biology and environment (the "fixed" mindset), you are right. If you think you are free to choose independently of your biology and environment (the "growth" mindset), you are also right.[28]

Yes, many scientific experts deny free will, but as John Tierney put it in the *New York Times*, "These supposed experts are deluding themselves if they think the question has been resolved. Free will hasn't been disproved scientifically or philosophically. The more that researchers investigate free will, the more good reasons there are to believe in it."[29] Agency is, by definition, outside the realm of cause and effect that governs the material world. Theologian Reinhold Niebuhr reminded us that nature is the realm of necessity, while history (human action) is the realm of freedom.[30]

It is also difficult to square free will with materialist accounts of evolution. If survival value is the necessary precondition for all human traits, then free will could never have come about because it is decidedly disadvantageous for survival. If there were one course of action that would lead to greater survival and another that would lead to extinction, how could the ability to choose the course of extinction enhance survival?[31] A survival robot, following the pro-survival instructions handed it by DNA and random mutations, would have a far greater chance of perpetuating its selfish genes than would a free being, who could choose drug addiction, suicide, or any other self-destructive behavior. Being programmed

---

27   Shaun Nichols, "Experimental Philosophy and the Problem of Free Will," *Science* vol. 331, iss. 6023 (March 18, 2011), 1401–3; and Charles Duhigg, *Smarter, Faster, Better* (NY: Random House, 2016).

28   Dweck, *Mindset*.

29   John Tierney, "Do You Have Free Will? Yes, It's the Only Choice," *New York Times*, March 22, 2011, D1.

30   Niebuhr, *The Irony of American History* (NY: Charles Scribner's Sons, 1962).

31   Some atheists, such as Daniel Dennett, have recently tried to have both materialism and free will by arguing that freedom is a product of evolution, but since freedom is decidedly not material, this amounts to an argument for "immaterial materialism." Daniel Dennett, *Freedom Evolves* (NY: Viking, 2003).

for pro-survival behaviors is, by definition, far better for survival than freedom to engage in anti-survival behaviors. Freedom to do evolutionarily stupid things can't be more beneficial than being programmed to do evolutionarily smart things.

In Darwinism, characteristics only emerge and remain in the gene pool when they help their possessor adapt and survive, but, as evolutionary theorist Robert Wright pointed out, "What is the survival value or adaptive function of self-consciousness and the freedom that comes with it?"[32] Accordingly, most atheists reject free will, and our culture is steadily following their lead. Belief in agency, sadly, is becoming ever-more-limited and our society is seeing many disturbing trends as a result.[33]

DEFAULTS AND OPT-OUTS

I suspect that a major reason people reject free will is because they have a mistaken conception of how it actually works. Too often, we have conceived of human freedom as the ability to make neutral, unbiased choices among competing alternatives. It's as if the chooser is free floating between multiple options and then, without constraint, choosing one (as if at random) over another.

Materialists have no problem knocking down this straw-man view of agency by pointing out the high correlation between genetics and environment, beliefs and behaviors. People born Catholic tend to remain Catholic, Mormons tend to remain Mormons, Democrats tend to remain Democrats, and Republicans tend to remain Republicans. If we were really free, wouldn't we see people from Mormon households choosing Catholicism just as often as they choose Mormonism?

Atheists seize on this fact and use it to denigrate the whole idea of free will. We don't make choices, they say—upbringing, peers, income level, schools, and DNA determine what we do. We are preprogrammed, says Harvard sociobiologist E. O. Wilson, to develop in a certain way—like Polaroid film—and then the environment determines on the margins

---

32   See final chapter of Robert Wright, *NonZero* (NY: Vintage, 2000).

33 Such as increasing rates of cheating and dishonesty among college students. See Tierney, "Do You Have Free Will? Yes, It's the Only Choice," D1.

whether we develop well or poorly.[34] In that sense, we are no different from ants acting according to roles programmed by DNA. We think we choose to be baptized into the LDS Church, join the Democratic Party, or show kindness to a stranger, but actually these affiliations and behaviors are chosen for us. In short, they say, free will is an illusion.

Now, at this point, a religious believer may come along and point out that, although we are constrained by genetics and environment, we have wiggle room within those constraints. The correlation between the economic status in which one is raised and in which one winds up is around 80 percent, then it would appear that we are free to choose the other 20 percent of our economic destiny. Yes, we inhabit a prison of biology and environment, but we can move around a little bit within this prison.

This view is also wrong. Agency doesn't operate on the principle of unconstrained or even constrained choice. It operates on the principles of *defaults* and *opt-outs*. Our genetics and environment provide us with default assumptions and behaviors, but we are entirely free to opt out of these defaults. For example, someone born Catholic will remain Catholic as a default, but they can, of course, choose to become something else. It's not that their upbringing chose 80 percent of their Catholicism—it chose 100 percent of it—but they are also 100 percent free to choose another religion. A person born into a Republican family will remain a Republican unless they make a conscious choice to go in a different direction. We aren't free because we are unconstrained by genetics and environment; we are free because we can opt out of our genetic and environmental defaults.

Social scientists have argued, using studies of identical twins raised in different households, that genetics determine a person's political views. Twins are far more likely to hold the politics of their twin than they are the politics of the family that raised them. This, they argue, shows that we are not nearly as much in control of our political choices as we like to think; our politics are up to 60 percent a function of DNA.[35]

---

34   For an entertaining exposition of Wilson's views, see Tom Wolfe, *Hooking Up* (NY: Farrar, Straus, and Giroux, 2000).

35   For a summary of this research, see Avi Tuschman, "Can Your Genes Predict Whether You'll Be a Conservative or a Liberal? Scientific research shows political partisanship transcends economics, environment, and upbringing," *The Atlantic*, October 24, 2013, accessed January 31, 2017, available at www .theatlantic.com/politics/archive/2013/10/can-your-genes-predict-whether -youll-be-a-conservative-or-a-liberal/280677/.

But look a bit closer: there is one person in the world who has more DNA in common with you than even your identical twin—yourself. And we find people completely changing their own political views all the time. It's not that they change them only up to 40 percent. They often change them 100 percent—a complete reversal. Communists become capitalists, democratic socialists become neoconservatives, Democrats become Republicans, Republicans become Democrats, and Democrats and Republicans become independents.[36] We are all born with a political default, but we can 100 percent choose to opt out of it. Those studies that claim "60 percent of politics are determined by genetics" would more accurately say that "60 percent of people do not choose to opt out of their political defaults."

Far from being the wiggle room we have within the prison of genetics and environment, free will can dominate *over* genetics and environment. Nature and nurture can shape and determine our lives as defaults, but we, as free beings, can consciously stand against them. Default is not destiny.

As an example of agency at work, think of fasting. The default behavior on a normal Sunday is to eat the delicious food available in the kitchen, but fasting itself is choosing to opt out of this default. Any other animal would simply follow the instinct to eat food set before it.[37] Humans, with the capacity to choose, are not destined to follow their biology. The environment (a delicious breakfast) provides us with the temptation (default), but with agency we can deny the temptation and fast (opt out).

While the Lord asks us to "put off the natural man" (Mosiah 3:19) and take responsibility for our actions, the world teaches us to follow our base instincts like any other object. The Lord tells us to opt out of our ungodly animal defaults, but the world tells us this is impossible since our animal natures define and determine who we are and who we will become. By following the world and failing to act as a "cause," we become an acted upon "effect."[38] Free will is under attack, and atheism is on the

---

36 For classic accounts of such intellectual journeys, see Peter Steinfels, *The Neoconservatives* (NY: Simon & Schuster, 1979); and John P. Diggins, *Up From Communism* (NY: Columbia University Press, 1975).

37 Unless conditioned through rewards or punishments to do otherwise.

38 This point is reinforced by the idea, recently popularized in works like Malcolm Gladwell's *The Tipping Point* (Boston: Little, Brown, and Company, 2000),

rise because it gives license to indulge our animal natures—if we are not free, then we are not responsible for any of our sinful behaviors. The denial of free will is one of the adversary's greatest tools to get us to surrender our virtue since it denies that virtue is even possible (there can be no virtuous choices without the ability to choose).

Understanding agency in terms of defaults and opt-outs also helps us refute some of the recent scientific arguments against free will. Jerry Coyne claims that because "brain scans can often predict the choices one will make several seconds before the subject is conscious of having chosen," choice itself must be an illusion.[39]

But Coyne is drawing a mistaken conclusion from the evidence. The study he cites only confirms something we've known for a long time: that there is a stimulus-response pattern associated with every choice. Brain scans can tell us that there is an environmental stimulus that serves as the default, but, as Coyne's cautious language makes clear, people often do not follow the stimulus default. Exercising free will doesn't mean you are independent of stimuli but only that there is a gap between stimulus and response in which opt-outs take place. The scientific studies Coyne cites only show that we can know stimuli in advance of choice. That's hardly a breakthrough, and it hardly weakens the case for free will.

While brain science hasn't refuted the idea of free will, recent findings in genetics are actually bolstering it. For years, scientists saw DNA as a kind of computer code that we, the biological computers, would execute. More recent studies, though, suggest that genes aren't so much like programs that control us but rather like books in a vast library that we can choose to access and activate through choices.[40] There are people who have alcoholic genes, yet they live and die without ever taking a drink. They never open the "alcoholic book" in their genetic library. Since choices and

---

that social trends operate like biological diseases. We "catch" the memes of our environment as they spread. But Gladwell fails to realize that, unlike biological diseases, we can choose whether or not to become infected. For example, if the trend of getting tattoos spreads like an epidemic, you nonetheless have the choice to "opt out" of this societal trend and remain tattoo-free.

39 Coyne, "Free Will," in *This Idea Must Die*, 154.

40 See, for example, Michael Purdy, "The Weird, Weird World of DNA," *Johns Hopkins Magazine* (November 2001), 53:5.

environment can unleash certain instincts, it seems that not only can we opt *out* of defaults, but we can also opt *in* to them. Genetics and free will, in that sense, harmonize quite well together.

An analogy to help us understand free will is river rafting. We are all born floating down the river of our genetics and environment. If we do nothing, we drift along wherever the current takes us. But we can choose to exit the river and enter another one. The river is the *default*; the choice to enter a different river is the *opt-out*.

Now, contrary to what some may say, there is no "objective viewpoint" from which to make our choices. We are always floating down one river or another. Nobody stands outside of all currents to see things from an unbiased perspective (as some critics of the Church claim). Choices are always made from a particular context. There is no neutral ground.

This is why critical examination is an essential principle of science and the gospel. While we are born with certain beliefs (defaults), we choose to stay in or opt out of them by subjecting them to criticism. There is nothing wrong with remaining in the religious, political, or other worldviews in which you were raised, so long as you have examined those beliefs, subjected them to scrutiny, and found them worth keeping. It's not a problem that a person born Mormon remains Mormon, but it is a problem that a person born Mormon doesn't choose to remain Mormon by gaining a testimony of their own through critical examination.

The river analogy also helps illuminate why so many have left the Church in recent years. The days are over when you could live your life simply floating down the river of Mormonism without conviction. There are now too many challenges to the default Mormon position—too many alternative rivers, easily accessed and inviting you to enter.

Being a mere "cultural Mormon," then, has become nearly impossible. If someone hasn't subjected the gospel to critical examination and gained a personal testimony, then they only remain in the Church by default and are subject to being blindsided by controversial aspects of Church history or the imperfections of Church leaders. As information becomes increasingly available, these people leave the Church because they never really chose to be part of it in the first place—it was simply their default. Members must gain testimonies for themselves and thereby consciously *choose* their faith. It can no longer be a matter of convenience.

I expect that in the future we will see a continuation of this trend as lukewarm members of the Church continue to be drawn to other rivers, while those who do remain in the river of the gospel will be stronger than ever, for their faith will have been tried and consciously chosen.

POLITICAL IMPLICATIONS

A correct understanding of agency also has crucial implications for political freedom. If we deny the reality of agency, we cannot expect liberty to survive, since, from a materialist point of view, humans are already "controlled" by genetics and environment. The logical outcome of materialism is totalitarianism.

Atheists generally champion the free inquiry that makes science possible, yet on what metaphysical grounds can they do so if we are all mere biological machines who aren't really free in the first place? If, as materialists claim, humans are just puppets of genetics and environment without the ability to choose, what, exactly, would a totalitarian government take away? How could anyone take away freedom of speech if speech was never free? What problem is there to depriving someone of their freedom of belief if they were programmed to hold those beliefs? From the materialist point of view, we have no more reason to fear government taking away our liberty than we have to fear government taking away our unicorns—both are fictitious.

Inasmuch as atheistic naturalism abolishes the distinction between the natural and the human, it also abolishes the distinction between control and freedom. Political freedom has long meant freedom from the coercions of other people (including governments), not freedom from nature. For instance, if an infection attacked my vocal cords, rendering me unable to speak, few would say I had been deprived of free speech. But if a policeman imprisoned me for saying something unpopular, we would agree that my free speech rights had been violated. How can we uphold that distinction if there is *no essential difference* between people and nature? If the policeman is every bit as "natural" as the infection, how could the atheist protest the policeman any more than the infection? Materialism offers no basis from which to resist a tyrannical government—there is no tyranny, for there is no real freedom for the government to take away.

And it's not just tyranny that we must fear under a materialist paradigm but also anarchy. Our system of laws that protects us from theft, murder, and other oppressions depends upon the punishment of persons for their crimes. But in the materialist view, people never choose to do wrong. Criminals are mere robots following programming, so we can't hold them accountable for their actions. Without freedom there is no responsibility. Both the sinner and saint neutrally follow their programming without ever making a choice to do right or wrong.

Materialism also destroys the Lockean arguments for freedom that the United States is based upon. If there is no "nature's God," as the Declaration of Independence puts it, then we have no entitlement to natural rights, for we have no intrinsic freedom to protect. Why protect a right to vote if you are merely programmed to vote for certain candidates or policies? Under materialism, American-style freedom can have no basis, and the Declaration of Independence is a meaningless piece of paper.

For all of the errors Karl Marx made, he was at least consistent in his materialism. He ridiculed American liberties as false "bourgeois freedoms." And since people in democratic capitalism weren't really free anyway, he said, why not create a society in which we trade an illusion—freedom of choice—for the comfort and equality of communism? Under materialist philosophy, he has a point.

Unlike Marx, many current-day atheists want to have it both ways. They reject the reality of human freedom as an illusion but at the same time proclaim their commitment to free choice (particularly when it comes to abortion), free inquiry, and a free society. Perhaps they are either pretending to believe in freedom when they don't or are too timid to take their convictions to their logical conclusion. Many atheists are happy to trumpet certain implications of their materialism (for example, no restrictions against hedonism), but are conspicuously silent when it comes to other implications (a society without freedom of speech).

Some atheists have tried to work around this problem by drawing a distinction between free will and determinism. We aren't free, they say, but that doesn't mean we just have to sit back and let things happen. We should still take steps to prevent a bad fate from befalling us. In other words, we have a determined free will.

Once again, these atheists aren't addressing the issue but only playing with words. Speaking of determined free will is a contradiction, on par with speaking of square circles or married bachelors. If we are determined, we are not free, and if something is logically impossible, then spilling mountains of ink in making sophisticated arguments to the contrary can't change that. The compatabilist view, which says that free will and determinism can harmonize, is untenable, and atheists can only make it seem otherwise by multiplying words (see Ecclesiastes 10:14).[41]

Either we have free will or we don't. If we are without will, then we are powerless to change what our fate will be (making fatalism correct), or we have free will in which case we can change our fate (making fatalism false).

A mathematician once used extensive, complicated math calculations to prove that 1 = 2. Other mathematicians with PhDs found the errors in his calculations, but even those of us who couldn't understand the math still knew, simply by the illogic of what he claimed to "prove," that his reasoning was false. Similarly, we need not understand the convoluted, opaque arguments of compatibilism to know that it is also false.

Unlike atheism, the LDS view provides strong metaphysical foundations for political freedom. The gospel tells us we are free beings created in the image of God. We are *subjects* fundamentally different from unfree material *objects* and righteous governments are sanctioned by God to protect that essential aspect of our nature. Doctrine and Covenants 134:1–2 teaches, "We believe that governments were instituted of God for the benefit of man [to] secure to each individual the free exercise of conscience, the right and control of property, and the protection of life." These rights are extensions of our agency, and our agency sets us apart from all else in nature, giving us an ontological[42] basis for political liberty.

Recognizing the connection between agency and political freedom, prophets have long taught that Latter-day Saints would have a crucial role in preserving the Constitution and free principles when they come under attack in the last days. As the world slides ever farther toward a materialist paradigm, the world's inhabitants will increasingly believe that freedom is an illusion and will happily surrender that freedom in the name of national greatness, security, equality, comfort, self-fulfillment, economic growth, or some other high-sounding ideal coming from political ideologues of right or left. Far too few of us have stopped to think how deeply

---

41 Most translations of this passage read, "The fool multiplies words." Christ's Apostles in the New World, by contrast, "did not multiply many words" (3 Nephi 19:24).

42 See chapter 8 for more on the meaning of the word *ontology*.

a free society depends upon a religious worldview. This must change if liberty in the world is to survive.[43]

CONCLUSION

Atheistic materialism has weak explanations for mind, weak explanations for the most basic and foundational facts of existence, and no ability to justify a free political order. It is not only a lame philosophy but a dangerous one.

The materialist paradigm also crumbles under the strain of contrary evidence as neuroplasticity, the placebo effect, quantum theory, and myriad other observable phenomena that disprove the materialist hypothesis. Those atheists who work vigorously to come up with creative explanations to save their materialism are a bit like Ptolemy's disciples who couldn't give up the geocentric universe model and invented epicycles to account for falsifying evidence. Atheists today are inventing epicycles in the brain to save their materialism.

In the name of honesty and simplicity, some atheists are finally throwing in the towel and conceding that materialism is untenable. Thomas Nagel, a distinguished New York University philosopher and atheist, recently argued that mind must be a fundamental property of the universe that exists uncreated alongside matter.[44] This is remarkably close to what we learn in the Pearl of Great Price and Doctrine and Covenants about intelligence. Thoughtful philosophers are just now arriving at truths taught over a century ago by an unlearned farm boy prophet.

A fish, if could it think and communicate, might swim about and glibly ask, "What water?" Atheists today glibly ask, "What spirit?" But even their act of intentionally speaking those words confirms the reality

---

43 The relationship between religion and freedom well explains why there is often a correlation between atheism and statism (government control over individual action). It's true that there have always been theocratic societies, but the atheistic societies premised on the materialist philosophy of Karl Marx have been the most statist of all. It's no wonder that statist political philosophies also dominate among the least religious sectors of American society (the media, entertainment, and the universities). Metaphysics matter, and materialist metaphysics matters for freedom.

44 Thomas Nagel, *Mind & Cosmos: Why the Materialist Neo-Darwinian Conception of Nature Is Almost Certainly False* (NY: Oxford University Press, 2012).

of what they deny. Consciousness and free will are the foreground and framework of all human activity, and they are all the proof we need of the reality of the spiritual.

In that sense, we need not look for God in the dark corners of the universe. We find Him in every thought we have, every decision we make, and every mental event we experience. The proof of the spiritual that the atheists seek is right before them, every moment. Still, they "have eyes but will not see" this obvious truth (Jeremiah 5:21).

Chapter 4

ATHEISM AND KNOWLEDGE

FALSE EPISTEMOLOGY

Most of the ultimate disagreements between people come down to this central question: how do you know? This makes epistemology—the study of knowing—central to every question, including the question of God's existence. Atheists arrive at many mistaken positions because they have a mistaken view of how one gains knowledge: incorrect epistemology leads them to incorrect conclusions.

Many thinkers in previous centuries believed that truth was something that sat around in nature in all of its purity, just awaiting discovery. All humans had to do was use reason to cut through superstition and tradition to get at this absolute, final truth.[1] For many, truth was like a valuable nugget of gold, waiting to be found and cherished.[2]

This view was limited. Today, most of us have come to realize that all truth is seen through various perspectives that lead different people to different views of reality. Although there is such a thing as absolute truth, we don't ever have unmediated sensory access to it—truth is filtered through our subjective perspectives. Even scientific theories are human creations embedded in man-made paradigms. They emerge from contextualized

---

1   The vocabulary of this paradigm is still with us inasmuch as we talk about scientific "discovery," a word which implies that truth merely needs to be uncovered.

2   Daniel Roche, *France in the Age of Enlightenment* (Cambridge: Harvard University Press, 1998), 88–89; and Leslie A. Murray, *Liberal Protestantism and Science* (Westport, CT: Greenwood, 2007), 9–11.

problems, experiences, and even prejudices. It's not that truth is relative, but that human *viewpoints* are relative. As the Apostle Paul said, those living in mortality "see through a glass darkly" (1 Corinthians 13:12).

These epistemic limitations (limits to knowledge) mean that, although science can come up with better models that are *closer* to the truth, these models are never final. Scientific truths are always contingent and open to revision as further findings and experiments add to our understanding and new paradigms replace old ones.

Despite the faults of those in my own field, historians were among the earliest to recognize the role that human subjectivity plays in scholarly inquiry. Unlike scientific materialists, historians acknowledged early on that objectivity was impossible and that our personal commitments and desires had a huge impact on historical interpretations. American Historical Association President Carl Becker even proclaimed in his inaugural address that writing history was "an act of faith."[3] Historical facts are always interpreted in light of the preconceptions and biases that historians bring to them. The same is true of all other areas of inquiry, including the hard sciences.

Few scholars today would dispute this view of epistemology, yet many atheists are still mired in the eighteenth-century view of absolute, unmediated scientific truth. They continue to view themselves as objective and religious believers as subjective (biased). As evidence, atheists point out that most religious believers tend to remain within the religious traditions into which they were born. This proves, they say, that believers merely perpetuate cultural prejudices inherited from their family and environment. You are a Latter-day Saint, the atheist would say, only because you were born one.

Now, putting aside the obvious fact that millions of Latter-day Saints were *not* born into the faith (including many of you reading this book), this argument fails to acknowledge that the truth of a position is independent of the *origin* of that position. To say otherwise is to fall prey to the genetic fallacy, which attempts to delegitimize a belief based on its source. Having been born and raised with certain beliefs says nothing about the correctness of those beliefs. "Truth is independent" (D&C 93:30) and does not rest upon any external factors, including upbringing. An idea has to be evaluated on its own merits and not dismissed simply because of who holds the position or how they came to it.

---

3   See Peter Novick, *That Noble Dream* (NY: Cambridge University Press, 1988).

While atheists use the genetic fallacy to try to invalidate religious beliefs, they fail to realize that it would also invalidate most of their *own* cherished beliefs. For instance, many atheists grew up in democratic countries. Does this fact delegitimize democracy? Hardly. If Mormons only believe in Mormonism because they were born into a Mormon society, then democrats only believe in democracy because they were born into a democratic society. It's wrong to say that growing up in a belief system somehow invalidates that belief system.

Given this inevitability of bias, how do we discern between competing views? How do we know which theories to accept and which to reject? Science, properly conceived, understands that beliefs are legitimized by *subjecting them to testing* (attempts at falsification). Science is not about going out and finding pure truth; it is about creating theories based on observation and holding them up to critical examination. Einstein found Newton's theory wanting and developed a new, more adequate one that we call general relativity. Astronomers tested the theory's core prediction during an eclipse and found that it came to pass. This corroborated the theory and made it an improvement over Newton's.

This is precisely what those with testimonies do with the gospel. A testimony does not come by being born into a Mormon family but by subjecting the gospel to critical examination and asking "if these things are not true" (Moroni 10:4). It was through critical inquiry, after all, that Joseph Smith came to have the First Vision that led to the Restoration itself. James 1:5 told him to "ask of God" to gain wisdom and that's what he did, even though what he learned in the Sacred Grove directly contradicted his upbringing and received traditions.

The important question is not whether I was born a Mormon but whether I put Mormonism to the test. I have. It passed. I continue to believe in it for the same reasons that I continue to believe the earth is round or that democracy is the best form of government. That I was born into a round-earth and democratic culture does not affect the correctness of a belief in a round earth or democracy; that I was born into a Mormon culture does not affect the correctness of Mormonism.

Contra the atheists, then, Mormons are no more dupes blindly going along with tradition than anyone else. If a Church member has acquired a testimony of the gospel in the same way that most people born in democracies come to believe in the goodness of democracy, then a belief in the gospel is as valid as a belief in democracy. I've never heard of an American

rejecting democracy because they felt they were brainwashed by a democratic family, but I have heard of Mormons rejecting the gospel because
they felt they were brainwashed by a Mormon family. The reasoning in
both cases is the same.

Another manifestation of the genetic fallacy is the atheist claim that
humans create God in their own image. Religious people, says the atheist, tend to project their own views and perspectives onto their divini-
ties. Even the ancient Greek historian Herodotus saw that the Greeks
worshipped Greek-looking Gods with Greek characteristics while Egyp-
tians worshipped Egyptian-looking gods with Egyptian characteristics.
Genesis had it backwards, says the atheist: God didn't create us in His
image; rather, we create Him in *our* image.

But what the atheist doesn't realize is that this point is utterly irrelevant to God's reality and nature. Andrew Ferguson has noted in his
impish book *Land of Lincoln* that Americans tend to create an Abraham
Lincoln who fits their own image. Conservatives claim that Lincoln was
conservative, liberals that Lincoln was liberal, depressives that Lincoln
was depressive, gays that Lincoln was gay, and so on. But this obviously
has nothing to do with Lincoln's actual characteristics or existence.[4]
Why would it be any different with God?

Robert Wright's *The Evolution of God* argues that over time, human
conceptions of God have evolved. With each passing generation, humans
have come to see God as less vindictive, provincial, and angry and more
tolerant, universal, and loving. Some atheists use the "evolution of God"
thesis to argue that He doesn't exist—what kind of a deity would change
to fit the times?

But what they fail to see is that God hasn't evolved; only our *understanding* of Him has. This is to be expected and is exactly how science
works. We have a changing view of the universe even though the truths
of the universe always have been and always will be independent of that
understanding. And if our understanding of all other fields improves with
further inquiry, why can't our understanding of God improve as well? To
say God doesn't exist because our view of Him has changed is as reckless
as saying the laws of physics don't exist because our view of them has
changed. We update science to fit our greater knowledge of the physical
world, and we update religion to fit our greater knowledge of God. That's

---

4   Andrew Ferguson, *Land of Lincoln* (NY: Grove, 2007).

why the fulness of the gospel was given in the fulness of times and modern prophets are necessary guides as we gain further light and knowledge of our Creator. If we have come to see God as more compassionate and tolerant and less brutal and violent, then this is merely an improvement in our *understanding* of God, not in God himself.[5]

Notice also that the New Atheists do precisely what they charge believers with doing: making up a God who suits their purposes. The God atheists attack is a straw man, easily knocked down by weak arguments: He is a cosmic genocidal maniac (in Richard Dawkins's words) who should be discoverable by science as a hypothesis (in Victor Stenger's words) and doesn't require any searching or change of behavior to come to a knowledge of Him.[6] Does that sound like a God anybody actually worships? The God the atheists *dis*believe in is far more a creation of human imagination than is the God Latter-day Saints *actually* believe in.

We see in politics how ideologues create caricatures of their opponents that are easy to knock down ("liberals hate America" or "conservatives hate the poor"), but atheists do the same in setting up a hollow God without any of the glory, majesty, or intelligence that we Latter-day Saints ascribe to Him. The real God of real believers is far more difficult to take on than the cosmic loser of Dawkins's imagination.[7]

EMPIRICIST DOGMATISM

The biggest atheist epistemological mistake of all is assuming that empiricism is the *only* way to gain knowledge. The atheist claims, without any justification, that we can *only know those things we find out through the*

---

5   God also may act differently throughout history not because He changes but because He needs to respond to different groups of His children in different ways. We parent two-year-olds different from sixteen-year-olds, and God may have "parented" the ancient Israelites differently than he "parents" twenty-first-century Americans.

6   See Dawkins, *The God Delusion*, chapter 2; and Victor J. Stenger, *God: The Failed Hypothesis* (Amherst, NY: Prometheus, 2008), foreword by Christopher Hitchens.

7   See Mary Eberstadt, *The Loser Letters* (San Francisco: Ignatius Press, 2010).

senses.[8] If we can see, hear, or touch something, we can have knowledge of it, but any other claims to knowledge are illegitimate. Atheists assert with full confidence, along with Korihor, "Ye cannot know of things which ye do not see; therefore ye cannot know that there shall be a Christ" (Alma 30:15). Since faith is defined as a belief in the true but unseen (Hebrews 11:1), atheists consider faith the height of delusion.[9]

But on what grounds do the atheists make the claim that only the senses can give knowledge? What reasoning, evidence, or authority led them to this conclusion? The answer is *none.* They make narrow empiricism a core assumption of their worldview for no reason at all.

When you point this out to atheists, they may respond, "I don't believe you can get extrasensory knowledge because *I* have never gotten extrasensory knowledge." This is tantamount to a blind person saying, "I don't think anyone can see because *I* have never seen." Atheists, in other words, are using their own spiritual deficiencies as evidence against spirituality in general. It's an attempt to impose their own limitations and narrow experiences onto everyone else—a form of bigotry.

If I close my eyes, I still know my wife exists because I remember seeing her before I closed them. But what if I was born blind and had never seen her? I would still know she exists through my other senses. If someone said, "No, you can't know your wife exists through your other senses because only sight counts," we would laugh them off as ridiculous. And yet that, in essence, is what the atheists do when they declare, for no reason, that only empirical evidence is valid.

This empiricist rejection of faith is not only unjustified, but it is also self-refuting. The claim "we can only believe what we see" *is itself based upon faith*, for there are no empirical grounds for believing that only empiricism gives knowledge. In other words, the idea that we can only know things through the senses, so central to atheism, is itself not known through the senses. If I say, "There is a house on top of that hill," I can verify the statement by climbing the hill and looking to see if a house is there. But the statement, "We can only know things through the senses" can find no such verification—it can only be taken on faith.

---

8   Dawkins, *The God Delusion*, 34–35, 45.

9   Harris, *End of Faith*, 12–15.

Atheists don't hold empiricism up for falsification (as true scientists would) but use it as the basis for everything else they believe. No atheist has ever "found out" that empiricism was true; they simply assumed it was and proceeded from there. Atheists declare that all non-empirical experiences are out of bounds as sources of knowledge, but this declaration is based on nothing but prejudice. There is no reason or justification for it, yet it remains at the core of the atheist critique of religion. When someone clings to a belief in such a way that no amount of evidence can convince them it's wrong, it is a *dogma*. One of the great ironies of atheism is that the atheist rejects faith for faith-based (dogmatic) reasons.

The influential philosopher W. V. O. Quine understood this. He turned away from his early logical positivism—the dominant empiricist philosophy of the twentieth century—because he saw that empiricism couldn't justify itself. Empiricists, he noted, make a dogmatic, unempirical claim to justify their empiricism.[10] They ridicule all non-sensory propositions but then cling to a non-sensory proposition themselves. They believe without seeing, and such belief is, by definition, faith. If the atheist can't believe in God because he hasn't seen Him, then he can't believe in empiricism for the same reason.

Even one of the central figures of logical positivism, Ludwig Wittgenstein, later found himself at odds with the philosophy, seeing that there was no basis for claiming that only empirical statements can lead to knowledge. So decisive was his turn from the dogmatic empiricism of his disciples that scholars today must distinguish between the early Wittgenstein—a major inspiration for logical positivism—and the late Wittgenstein—a Christian mystic.[11]

Like Quine and Wittgenstein, most great thinkers have realized that the simplistic empiricism of the atheists is unjustified and based on wishful thinking—the very thing that atheists say is at the root of most religious belief. Yet the New Atheists continue to cling to their dogmatic

---

10 Willard Van Orman Quine, "The Two Dogmas of Empiricism," *The Philosophical Review* vol. 60 (1951), 20–43.

11 Wittgenstein's *Tractatus Logico-Philosophicus* (1921) is widely seen as the text that launched the Vienna Circle, the group that disseminated logical positivism as a dominant philosophy in the western world. The *Tractatus* brought many to the idea that knowledge is embodied in language that logically "pictures" empirical reality.

empiricism, unaware of how thoroughly it has been debunked. Like a six-day creationist, the atheist holds to his faith without regard for reason or evidence. He has become the unwitting zealot of a secular religion.

Although empiricism is a dogma, there is nothing wrong with dogmas *per se*, since all of us have them and they constitute the starting points (rather than the ending points) of our inquiry. But to deny we have them is an act of intellectual dishonesty. Atheists claim to reject *all* dogmas—they are open-minded scientists, after all—but then sneak the empiricist dogma in through the back door, hoping that nobody will notice. Atheists are fond of calling the religious closed-minded, but, as their view on empiricism shows, there is a fundamental closed-mindedness at the heart of their atheism. They cling tightly to their empiricist faith all the while ridiculing the idea of faith itself.

Unlike atheists, Latter-day Saints admit that faith is central to what we believe. Our convictions do not just jump out to us in their purity; we *choose* to believe them. Atheists choose a faith in empiricist materialism, while Latter-day Saints choose a faith in Christ. Both are faiths, but Latter-day Saints admit theirs; atheists do not.

REVELATION

While atheists are stuck with the self-refuting empiricist dogma that there is one—and only one—path to truth, Latter-day Saints have a flexible and balanced epistemology that allows us to gather truth from the senses as well as from revelation (which includes promptings of the Holy Ghost, inspiration, impressions, moral intuitions, and truths revealed through prophets). We can gain knowledge by study *and* faith. By study we gain empirical knowledge; by faith we receive revelation. We are grounded in eternal truth (dogmas) through revelation but also open to contingent truth (such as scientific theories) through the senses. Elder Richard G. Scott, himself a scientist, summarized LDS epistemology: "There are two ways to find truth—both useful, provided we follow the laws upon which they are predicated. The first is the scientific method [but] the best way of finding truth is simply to go to the origin of all truth and ask."[12]

---

12 Richard G. Scott, "Truth: The Foundation of Correct Decisions," *Ensign*, November 2007.

The difference between science and revelation is not only one of method, but it's also a difference in the *kind* of knowledge received. Science yields knowledge that is contingent and open to revision. Karl Popper pointed out that our scientific theories are, indeed, artificial—we make them up through creative acts of imagination—but that doesn't mean they have no truth value, since more accurate theories hold up to our attempts to falsify them through testing. We have no way to know if a scientific theory is true, but we can know if it is false and can thereby advance to better theories. Science is not the search for final truth but the search for *more* truth.

Revelation, on the other hand, can yield ultimate truth—ultimate because the truths can be final (absolute) and ultimate because they are concerned with that which is most important in life (love, beauty, freedom, morals, and meaning). Science has nothing to say on these matters, but revelation does. Hence, it is, in Elder Scott's words, "the best way of finding truth." We know through the witness of the Holy Ghost that the Book of Mormon is true. We know through moral intuition that it is wrong to torture innocents. We know through direct revelation the equal value of people of all races. We know intuitively that we exist. We know through feelings that we love our spouses and children. Science does not, nor could it ever, tell us these facts. We don't hold the knowledge of whom we love contingent, waiting for scientists to falsify it—that knowledge is beyond the possibility of scientific confirmation or refutation. The most important aspects of life, we can see, are outside the realm of science—they are matters for revelation.[13]

Even the atheist knows she loves her children, knows she exists, knows it's wrong to torture innocents, and knows racial prejudice is wrong. She doesn't hold these beliefs hostage to the caprices of science, yet that same atheist might castigate the religious for "naïvely" believing things they can't see.

Albert Einstein himself rightly noted this atheist mistake in his famous 1930 essay, "Religion and Science." He understood that some scientists

---

13 Many atheists reject revelation on the grounds that many frauds have claimed to have revelations to gain power or money, but there are charlatans trying to get power and money in every walk of life—including science. That certain frauds and quacks claim an epistemological method does not discredit the method. False science doesn't delegitimize science, and false revelation doesn't delegitimize revelation.

made a "fatal error" in their "attempt to arrive at fundamental judgments with respect to values and ends on the basis of scientific method." Instead of setting themselves "in opposition to religion," said Einstein, scientists should recognize that "science without religion is lame."[14] When it comes to the fact/value distinction, science has much to say about facts but nothing to say about values.

I happen to believe in the value of racial equality for religious reasons, but atheistic empiricists have no reasons for doing so. Nobody has ever seen the value of racial equality, so it is outside the domain of empiricism. On what grounds, then, can the dogmatic empiricist champion the equality of all peoples? If science discovered differences in ability or intelligence among the races, would atheists then throw out their belief in the equal value of all people? Would they be willing to discard this sacred moral commitment in the face of new evidence? Presumably not, and since no amount of scientific evidence would convince an atheist to become a racist, their belief in the equal dignity of all people is a dogma.

The ideas of equality, democracy, and human rights are as sacred to the atheist as any LDS doctrine is to a Mormon. Contrary to their own claims, atheists have dogmas, and their dogmas are nonempirical. This should be sufficient to put to rest the atheists' claim that they only accept sensory knowledge and will follow scientific evidence wherever it leads. Latter-day Saints freely accept that there are dogmas; the atheist, on the other hand, is in denial, clinging to the illusion that he only believes what he can see. Atheists profess an unjustified commitment to empiricism in theory and then constantly violate that commitment in practice.

We sometimes call the religious "people of faith," but the reality is that everyone, including atheists, are people of faith, for everyone believes in things they can't see. Science is about empirical falsification and nonfinal truth, yet there are nonempirical, final truths that even atheists accept because of a "desire to believe" (Alma 32:35). They differ from believers only in their refusal to acknowledge this faith.[15] President Boyd K. Packer

---

14 Albert Einstein, "Religion and Science," *New York Times Magazine* (November 9, 1930), 1–4.

15 Scottish philosopher David Hume (one of the few consistent atheists in history) pointed out that even our belief in such fundamental principles as causation and induction are dogmas, yet they are foundational to science. We have no empirical reason for believing in cause and effect (or even the idea of regularity and

taught, "There is a crying need for the identification of atheism for what it is, and that is, a religion."[16]

SOCIETY'S DOGMAS

Atheists look back on the Middle Ages as a benighted time when people believed things without scientific justification. Is our own age really that much different? *What* we consider dogmas has changed, but dogmas are still very much with us, as is the persecution of heretics who dissent from them.

A society's dogmas are revealed in its profanities. If you identify the taboo words of a culture, you will also have found what it holds sacred. A century ago, genteel Americans would casually utter racial slurs in public but never the curse words associated with God, the body, or sexuality. Today, it is the opposite. The n-word is considered a curse word for the *same reason* the f-word once was: it is a derogatory way to refer to something society holds sacred. We have appropriately increased our reverence for racial equality but have inappropriately decreased our reverence for God, sex, and the body.

Atheists often boast of a willingness to dissent and courageously challenge the sacred cows of society,[17] but if this is so, why do they only challenge those things that are popular to ridicule? For instance, *Skeptic* magazine editor Michael Shermer routinely makes fun of Latter-day Saint temple garments, but he would never ridicule Islam or the idea of racial equality in the same way. The consequences would be social ostracism, widespread condemnation, blacklisting, job loss, and perhaps even a fatwa. He faces no social consequences for mocking Mormon temple garments—on the contrary, it gets him applause and laughter—but there are severe consequences for mocking racial equality or Islam.

---

uniformity in nature), but we do so anyway as a matter of faith. "Nondogmatic" science, it would appear, can't even work without dogmas.

16 Boyd K. Packer, "What Every Freshman Should Know," *Ensign*, September 1973, accessed November 15, 2016, available at www.lds.org/ensign/1973/09/what-every-freshman-should-know?lang=eng.

17 See, for example, Sam Harris, *The Moral Landscape: How Science Can Determine Human Values* (NY: Simon & Schuster, 2010), 24.

Shermer is hardly courageous when he only criticizes things that are safe to disparage.

Many atheists have also joined in persecuting those who don't fall in line with the dogma of gay marriage. How is their behavior procedurally different from that of medievalists who persecuted dissenters from Christianity? Both are examples of compelling people to accept society's dominant paradigm. Atheists often applaud Galileo's brave decision to challenge the dogmas of the seventeenth-century Catholic Church, but they themselves won't challenge the dogmas of twenty-first-century "secular progressivism."[18]

A correct epistemology also falsifies the common atheist claim that religious believers are arrogant for thinking they belong to the true religion.[19] If revelation is a valid source of knowledge, then it is no more arrogant for a religious believer to claim he knows through revelation that the Church is true than it is for a scientist to claim he knows through science that evolution is true. And just as it is not arrogant for a scholar to try to persuade others to accept evolution (as I've tried to do in this book), so it is not arrogant for a Mormon to try to persuade others to accept the gospel (as I've also tried to do in this book).

Understanding the distinction between contingent, empirical truth and final, revelatory truth also helps us untangle one of the great philosophical disputes that has divided thinkers for decades. In the late 1940s, after the horrors of World War II, the Holocaust, and Stalin's gulags, a question highly debated among intellectuals arose: should we be absolutist and believe in final truths, or should we be relativist and believe in contingent truth? Absolutists and relativists both accused the other side of being totalitarians. If we don't have absolute convictions, said one side, how can we fight evils such as Nazism or Communism? The other side

---

18   Dennett, *Breaking the Spell*, 53. New Atheist Christopher Hitchens is a notable
      exception to this rule. Against "progressive" opinion, he opposed abortion rights,
      which cost him his job at *The Nation* magazine. He also supported the war in
      Iraq long after a majority of Americans had turned against it. Although I may
      disagree with many of Hitchens's political positions (especially on foreign policy),
      I applaud his independence of mind and willingness to buck the orthodoxies of
      both "left" and "right."

19   See, for example, Dennett, *Breaking the Spell*, 51.

responded that it's absolutism itself that creates Nazis and Communists, so our relativism is what sets us apart from them.[20]

As is often the case, both sides in the debate were partially right and partially wrong. There is both a realm of certainty (dogma) and a realm of uncertainty (empiricism). We should be relativist (tentative with findings) when it comes to empirical knowledge, but we should be absolutist and unwavering when it comes to revealed knowledge (dogmas). Leave contingent those findings that are contingent (the latest theory on the origin of life), but hold certain those truths that are certain (the wrongness of genocide).

Thomas Jefferson well articulated this synthesis of the two sources of knowledge in the Declaration of Independence. The Scottish common-sense tradition taught Jefferson that there were some absolute, final truths we know without sensory evidence (the self-evident truths of equality and rights), while the English empirical tradition taught Jefferson that there are truths that we have to find out through the senses. By merging the Scottish common sense of Thomas Reid with the English empiricism of John Locke, Jefferson and the other Founding Fathers put forward a synthesis philosophy that recognized the value of both dogma and empiricism (rather than the dogma *of* empiricism that atheists subscribe to). We should, like the Founders, remain committed to eternal, unempirical truths but leave all other truths open to revision as science and experience lead us to change our minds.

So much for atheist empiricism. What about materialism? The same arguments against the empiricist dogma also apply to the materialist dogma. Atheists have declared, without any justification, that only material reality exists. But how did they come to this knowledge? Where is the evidence? There is none. Alma's words to Korihor might be said to today's atheists: "What evidence have ye that there is no God, or that Christ cometh not? I say unto you that ye have none, save it be your word only" (Alma 30:40).

Harvard geneticist Richard Lewontin is candid enough to admit this. In a 1996 article, he confessed that atheists like him have a prior commitment to materialism and that

---

20 For more, see Edward A. Purcell, Jr., *The Crisis of Democratic Theory* (Lexington: University Press of Kentucky, 1973); and Hyrum Lewis, "The Conservative Capture of Anti-Relativist Discourse in Postwar America," *Canadian Journal of History/Annales canadiennes d'histoire XLIII*, Winter/hiver 2008, 451–75.

It is not that the methods and institutions of science somehow compel us to accept a material explanation of the phenomenal world, but, on the contrary, that we are forced by our a priori adherence to material causes to create an apparatus of investigation and a set of concepts that produce material explanations, no matter how counter-intuitive, no matter how mystifying to the uninitiated. Moreover, that materialism is absolute, for we cannot allow a Divine Foot in the door.[21]

Since materialism is an assumption, not a conclusion, no scientific discovery would ever change the materialist's belief in materialism. It is, like their empiricism, a matter of faith. By definition, then, materialism can never be "scientific" materialism. As neuroscientist Mario Beauregard says of his colleagues, "Neuroscientists have not yet discovered [materialism]; they start their work with that assumption. Anything they find is interpreted on the basis of that view."[22]

DOGMAS AS FRAMES

We established earlier that everyone holds to dogmas, so the question for all people everywhere is not, "Should we have faith?" Instead it is, "What should we have faith in?" The choice of faith is especially important since it frames our other beliefs and choices—it provides the foundational starting point from which to interpret and evaluate all other experiences. The fourth article of faith makes clear that the first principle of the gospel is not just faith but faith *in Christ*. When we have chosen faith in Christ, rather than a false God (such as materialism, money, career, possessions, heroes, science, or ideology), millions of life choices follow.

We can see the framing power of faith at work in the realm of politics. Why can people on both the political left and right be equally rational and empirical yet disagree so stridently on policy? Milton Friedman and Paul Krugman were both Nobel Prize winners and distinguished economists at top universities, but they disagreed on nearly every point of politics because they had different dogmas as starting points. Neither was religious, but both had faith. Each adhered to underlying dogmas that

---

21   Richard Lewontin, "Billions and Billions of Demons," *New York Review of Books*, January 9, 1997, 31.

22   Mario Beauregard and Denyse O'Leary, *The Spiritual Brain: A Neuroscientist's Case for the Existence of the Soul* (NY: HarperOne 2008), 4.

preceded and framed their respective interpretations of empirical evidence. Krugman began with fairness as his nonempirical dogma, while Friedman began with freedom as his. Through faith, Krugman chose government intervention, and through faith, Friedman chose free markets. Through faith, two comparably smart economists came to opposite conclusions. The empirical truth of economics was not just out there awaiting discovery but was filtered through the dogmatic frameworks that each adopted. It's not that both dogmas were equally false, only that neither was fully justified through empiricism alone.

Turning political ideology into a faith can get quite ugly. Karl Marx offered one of the great faiths of human history—a full-blown atheistic religion with sacred texts (*Das Kapital* and *The Communist Manifesto*), prophets (Marx and Engels), ultimate salvation (the communist utopia), and heretics to punish (Trotsky and other dissidents). As Europeans became less religious in the twentieth century, their inclination to faith didn't go away; they just transferred it to the secular faiths of nationalism, fascism, and communism.[23] The conflicts between these secular faiths led to much of the violence and misery of the twentieth century.

CONCLUSION

Latter-day Saints understand that we can choose, via faith, to accept the validity of spiritual experiences or we can choose, via faith, to believe in scientific materialism. If we choose materialism as our faith, then spiritual experiences are just brain-produced hallucinations and all those who claim to have experienced God are either deluded or lying. Either way, what we choose to believe is wishful thinking. In both Mormonism and materialism, one makes a leap of faith into certain beliefs that are not justified by empirical evidence alone. The ubiquity of faith, then, must be recognized as not only inevitable but the reason for mortality.

Because we live by faith, the only question is, will our faith be determined by revelation or by passing fads? If people don't get their dogmas from God, they will simply absorb them from society or peer groups. But the world's faiths are fickle and unreliable: they led antebellum southerners to racism, Germans to Nazism, and current Americans to the whims

---

23 This is a point that some of the most famous Marxists later acknowledged. See Arthur Koestler, et. al., *The God that Failed* (NY: Harper & Row, 1963).

of ideological conservatism or progressivism. The trends of the world are as unsteady as the shifting sands. Rocks, by contrast, persist and hold steady. Christ is the rock. Since we must have faith in something, we should put our faith in Christ. Only He is worthy of it.

Chapter 5

ATHEISM AND TESTIMONY

In PURSUING KNOWLEDGE THROUGH REVELATION, Latter-day Saints seek a testimony above all else. At its most basic, a testimony is a belief in the truthfulness of the gospel. As with all justified dogmas, a testimony usually doesn't come through empirical inquiry (although that can help) but through spiritual witness. This is why materialist scientists, cheating in the game of "what is knowledge," reject the whole idea of testimony *a priori*. They have, without reason, declared spiritual witness to be illegitimate, making a testimony out of bounds from the get-go. But if we accept revelation as a valid means of gaining knowledge, then we can also accept that a testimony gained through the Spirit can be at least as justified as any sensory knowledge.

Many Mormons are fortunate enough to have a testimony that is absolutely certain—they have been given the gift of knowledge from God. Doubt, said Elder Bruce R. McConkie, was as foreign to him as the "gibberish of alien tongues."[1] He simply knew and had always known that the gospel was true. This certainty among so many Mormons is evidenced in monthly testimony meetings when members stand and publicly declare that they know the gospel is true.

---

1   Bruce R. McConkie, *The Promised Messiah* (Salt Lake City: Deseret Book, 1978), xvii. For more on certain testimony, see Jack R. Christianson and K. Douglas Bassett, *Life Lessons from the Book of Mormon* (Springville, UT: Cedar Fort, 2007), 219.

TESTIMONY OF OTHERS

Many members of the Church—perhaps even most—don't have this absolute certainty. Their gift is not that of knowledge but, instead, the gift of faith or the gift of believing on the words of others (see D&C 46:13–14). This means that many Mormons have a secondhand testimony of the gospel. They are like jury members in a courtroom who didn't witness an event but nonetheless believe in its reality because of the strong, sincere testimony of trustworthy witnesses. Just as a juror can know beyond a reasonable doubt that a defendant is guilty, so members can know beyond a reasonable doubt that the gospel is true by relying on the witness of others.

We shouldn't discount this secondhand testimony of the gospel. It is powerful. Elder Dallin H. Oaks appealed to those who had the gift of believing in the words of others in a 2011 address: "Modern revelation teaches that some have the gift 'to know that Jesus Christ is the Son of God, . . . crucified for the sins of the world,' and that it is given to others 'to believe on their words.' As one who knows, I invite you to believe on my words."[2]

For other members of the Church, gaining a testimony is a process. It is less like a light that is switched on or off and more like a seed that, when cultivated, undergoes steady, often imperceptible growth until it becomes full and perfect (see Alma 32). Knowledge, for such people, is the end result of the process of testimony, not the beginning.[3]

EMPIRICAL TESTIMONY

It's also possible to gain a testimony through actual sensory experience of God. Moses spoke with God face-to-face. Joseph Smith and Sidney Rigdon testified that Christ lived "for [they] saw Him" (D&C 76:23). The New Testament disciples saw and handled the resurrected

---

2   Dallin H. Oaks, "Truth and Tolerance," CES Devotional for Young Adults, September 11, 2011, Brigham Young University, accessed May 31, 2016, available at www.lds.org/broadcasts/article/ces-devotionals/2011/01/truth-and -tolerance?lang=eng.

3   See also Elder Bednar's video series, "Patterns of Light," accessed September 29, 2016, available at www.lds.org/media-library/video/2012-01-012-patterns-of -light-spirit-of-revelation?lang=eng,

Jesus (see Luke 24:39). Thousands of Nephites heard Christ's voice, saw Him descending from heaven, and finally went forward one by one to feel the wounds in His hands and feet (see 3 Nephi 10–11). David B. Haight, Lorenzo Snow, Joseph F. Smith, and other modern Apostles have seen Christ in visions. Similar reports by other Church members could fill volumes.

This sensory witness of God means that an open (rather than dogmatic) empiricism has an important place in the gospel. While the senses are not the only path to knowledge (contrary to what the atheists say), they are still a path and can even be a path to religious knowledge. Seeing God, seeing an angel, or seeing ancient golden plates all yield religious truth. The importance of Book of Mormon witnesses underscores this point.

Joseph Smith believed so much in the importance of sensory experience that he said, "No one can truly say he knows God until he has handled something, and this can only be in the Holiest of Holies."[4] Truman Madsen pointed out that when Christ appeared to His disciples after His death, He didn't say, "Go check out the arguments for God." Instead He said, "Handle me and see." Madsen, trained in the philosophical tradition of logical positivism, even concluded that a great strength of LDS belief was its "theological empiricism."[5]

NEAR-DEATH EXPERIENCES

Part of believing on the testimony of others includes accepting such empirical witnesses. Most of us will never have sensory knowledge of God in this life, and even today's Apostles and prophets, for the most part, remain silent about having seen God. And yet millions of people worldwide, most of them not of our faith, *do* report empirical experiences of God, usually in a near-death experience.

First made famous by Dr. Raymond Moody in his 1975 book *Life after Life*, near-death experiences (NDEs) are now a widely known, widely

---

4   Joseph Smith, discourse in Nauvoo, May 1, 1842, quoted in Andrew Jenson, ed., *The Historical Record*, vols. 5–8 (Salt Lake City: Andrew Jenson, 1889), 493.

5   For more on Madsen's empiricism, see his doctoral thesis, "A Philosophical Examination of Tillich's Theory of Symbolic Meaning," PhD diss., Harvard University, 1958.

reported, and widely studied phenomenon. Those who have experienced an NDE (I'll call them returners, since most of them would say they were beyond death and came back), report having left their bodies, traveled to a heavenly realm, and encountered a divine being of light that many of them identify as Jesus Christ.[6]

One might quibble with the word *empirical* used in this context. After all, if returners are not in their bodies, are their experiences of God even "sensory"? The returners sure think so. They claim that they were seeing, hearing, and feeling in an even more profound and real way than they ever had before. Their empirical experience of God, they say, was every bit as real as (indeed even more real than) their daily experiences on earth. People blind from birth even report, after an NDE, knowing what it is to see and can describe colors and objects in ways that were impossible before.[7]

It's remarkable how often the testimonies of returners support LDS doctrine. Wendy and Brent L. Top have done an in-depth study showing that Mormon beliefs are largely validated by NDEs.[8] Returners report continuing their existence in a spirit body, experiencing God as a being full of light, sensing the relativity of time, finding that family relationships

---

6   Leading LDS scholar Hugh Nibley, who knew Raymond Moody, also had an NDE that dispelled his doubts about life after death. See the BYU-produced documentary film, *The Faith of an Observer*. F. Enzio Busche of the First Quorum of the Seventy also had what appears to have been an NDE, reported in Busche, *Yearning for the Living God* (Salt Lake City: Deseret Book, 2004). For an unorganized series of LDS anecdotes of NDE's, see Lee Nelson, *Beyond the Veil* (Springville, UT: Cedar Fort, 2011). Apostle David B. Haight's experience with Christ has characteristics of an NDE. See David B. Haight, "The Sacrament— and the Sacrifice," *Ensign*, November 1989. Robert Fillerup has shown how closely Joseph Smith's First Vision parallels the near-death experience, including the initial darkness, seeing a being of light, undergoing a life review, receiving a communication of intelligence, and then being reluctant to share the experience with others. Fillerup is not claiming that the Prophet had an NDE, only that various spiritual experiences, whether in the Sacred Grove, or at the moment of death, may have commonalities. See Robert Fillerup, "Early Mormon Visions and Near-death Experiences," paper given at Sunstone Symposium, Salt Lake City, August 22, 1990.

7   Jeffrey Long, *Evidence of the Afterlife* (NY: HarperOne, 2010).

8   Brent L. and Wendy C. Top, *Glimpses Beyond Death's Door: Gospel Insights into Near-death Experiences* (Orem, UT: Granite Publishing, 2010).

continue beyond the grave, seeing an embodied Christ, feeling forgiveness for sins, understanding that they had a premortal life, and even seeing three degrees of glory—all which support elements of LDS doctrine (see sections 76, 130, and 131 of the Doctrine and Covenants).[9]

George Ritchie, a non-LDS soldier from Virginia, died of pneumonia in a Texas army hospital and then found himself with the resurrected Christ, being guided on a tour of a spirit world, and witnessing the process of eternal progression.[10] Much of what he saw in his experience is unique to LDS doctrine. Ritchie never converted to Mormonism but had great respect for LDS members and beliefs.[11]

Howard Storm, a former atheist college professor, converted to Christianity and became a minister after having a near-death experience that has striking parallels to Alma the Younger's vision. After dying in a French hospital, Storm reported his feelings as such:

> So ashamed of who I was, and what I had been all of my life, that all I wanted to do was hide in the darkness. The agony that I had suffered during the day was nothing compared to what I was feeling now. I knew then that this was the absolute end of my existence, and it was more horrible than anything I could possibly have imagined. Then a most unusual thing happened. I heard very clearly, once again in my own voice, something that I had learned in nursery Sunday School. It was the little song, "Jesus loves me, yes I know . . ." and it kept repeating. I don't know why, but all of a sudden I wanted to believe

---

9   See, for example, Eben Alexander, *Proof of Heaven* (NY: Simon & Schuster, 2012); Crystal McVea, *Waking Up in Heaven* (NY: Howard, 2013); Mary Neal, *To Heaven and Back* (Colorado Springs: WaterBrook, 2012); Sarah Menet, *There Is No Death* (Wheat Ridge, CO: Mountain Top, 2002); and Betty Eadie, *Embraced by the Light* (NY: Bantam, 1994). Eadie's experience so supported Mormon teachings that some have accused her of inventing her experience to propagandize for LDS beliefs (for example, Doug Groothuis, *Deceived by the Light* [Eugene, OR: Harvest House, 1995]). For summary see scholarly studies of near-death experiences, see Kenneth Ring, *Lessons from the Light* (Needham, MA: Moment Point Press, 2006); Pim van Lommel, *Consciousness Beyond Life* (NY: HarperOne, 2010); and Elisabeth Kübler-Ross, *On Life After Death* (NY: Celestial Arts, 1991).

10   George Ritchie, *Return from Tomorrow* (Grand Rapids, MI: Baker, 1978).

11   See Ritchie's foreword to Elane Durham, *I Stand All Amazed: Love & Healing from Higher Realms* (Orem, UT: Granite, 1998).

that. Not having anything left, I wanted to cling to that thought. And I, inside, screamed, "Jesus, please save me." That thought was screamed with every ounce of strength and feeling left in me. When I did that, I saw, off in the darkness somewhere, the tiniest little star. Not knowing what it was, I presumed it must be a comet or a meteor, because it was moving rapidly. Then I realized it was coming toward me. It was getting very bright, rapidly. When the light came near, its radiance spilled over me, and I just rose up—not with my effort—I just lifted up. Then I saw—and I saw this very plainly—I saw all my wounds, all my tears, all my brokenness, melt away. And I became whole in this radiance. What I did was to cry uncontrollably. I was crying, not out of sadness, but because I was feeling things that I had never felt before in my life.[12]

Compare this experience to that of Alma the Younger, who said:

And now, for three days and for three nights was I racked, even with the pains of a damned soul.

And it came to pass that as I was thus racked with torment, while I was harrowed up by the memory of my many sins, behold, I remembered also to have heard my father prophesy unto the people concerning the coming of one Jesus Christ, a Son of God, to atone for the sins of the world.

Now, as my mind caught hold upon this thought, I cried within my heart: O Jesus, thou Son of God, have mercy on me, who am in the gall of bitterness, and am encircled about by the everlasting chains of death.

And now, behold, when I thought this, I could remember my pains no more; yea, I was harrowed up by the memory of my sins no more.

And oh, what joy, and what marvelous light I did behold; yea, my soul was filled with joy as exceeding as was my pain! (Alma 36:16–20)

Given the sincerity of those who report near-death experiences and the strong overlap with LDS doctrines, members have every reason to welcome these accounts as yet more "words of knowledge" to bolster their testimonies.[13] Atheists, on the other hand, are stuck in quite a dilemma

---

12   Howard Storm, "Reverend Howard Storm's Near-Death Experience." Excerpted from his book *My Descent into Death*. Found at www.near-death.com/experiences /notable/howard-storm.html, accessed July 2, 2016.

13   Some Latter-day Saints might resist accepting the validity of NDE's because they are often lumped together with "new age," "fringe," and paranormal subjects,

when it comes to visions and NDEs. What do they do with these empirical experiences? How do they deal with the fact that millions of people worldwide, independently of one another, assert in all solemnity and sincerity that they have seen God?

MATERIALISTS EXPLAIN AWAY

Dogmatic atheists will attempt to reduce all of these supernatural experiences to fraud or brain science. For years, atheists would catalog heavenly visions with crackpot nonsense and hoaxes, such as sightings of Bigfoot, the Loch Ness monster, or UFOs. These purported after death stories, said the atheists, were just elaborate scams perpetrated by the conniving on the gullible.

This glib dismissal didn't hold up. Unlike those given to hoaxes, returners are overwhelmingly credible, honest people, usually highly respected in their communities and professions. Doctors, for whatever reason, seem especially high on the list—George Ritchie was a leading Virginia psychiatrist, Mary Neal was a professor of spinal surgery at USC, Eben Alexander was a Harvard neurosurgeon, and Elisabeth Kübler-Ross was a University of Chicago health scientist and creator of the famous "five stages of grief" model. These prominent physicians didn't recant under pressure or come out as frauds under further scrutiny. They had nothing to gain by presenting their stories and often had much to lose. In fact, most returners were highly reluctant to share their experiences for fear of ridicule—quite the opposite of publicity seeking phonies. Many returners have even submitted to and successfully passed polygraph tests to prove their honesty about their experiences.

Given the credibility and quantity of returners, atheists gave up trying to dismiss them as frauds and instead tried to discount NDEs by

such as psychic mediumship. But putting A into a category with B doesn't make the truth of A contingent on B. For instance, in the Republican Party there are "birther" conspiracy theorists, while in the Democratic Party there are "truther" conspiracy theorists. The association of "truthers" with, say, a policy of tax increases on the rich, does not discredit that policy. Also notice that Joseph Smith's revelations were often considered "quack" and "fringe" when first presented. It was his openness to experiences, regardless of their labels ("magic") or prejudices against them, that made him humble enough to restore the gospel in this dispensation. See Richard Bushman, *Joseph Smith and the Beginnings of Mormonism* (Urbana: University of Illinois Press, 1984).

calling them brain-produced delusions. Most returners, the atheist says, sincerely believe in the reality of their experiences, but it is actually just the product of a malfunctioning brain. The atheist points out that people on hallucinogenic drugs sometimes report experiencing the feelings of euphoria, calm and peace, being out of the body, or being at one with the Universe that are characteristic of NDEs. Some pilots in a state of oxygen deprivation at high altitudes have even reported seeing family members. Since drug users clearly don't experience any reality when they are tripping, says the atheist, returners are similarly not experiencing any reality when under the stress of being near death. It's just an illusion produced by the brain in a state of hypoxia or under chemical influence. We can, the atheist says, simply explain away near-death experiences by invoking brain science.

The same goes for any other claims of religious visions or spiritual manifestations. To the atheist, they aren't real and certainly aren't a valid way to gain knowledge. If you claim to know that God exists through personal spiritual witness, revelation, or vision, the atheist will counter that you only *think* you know those things—you are being tricked by your brain. For example, if you receive a spiritual witness that the Book of Mormon is true, rest assured that this is merely a brain-produced feeling. Your mind evolved to believe nonsense, so we can just discard your spiritual experiences accordingly.[14]

Atheists also point out that, by manipulating the brain's temporal lobe (sometimes by using a God Helmet—a device that stimulates the brain to produce mystical feelings), scientists have created pseudo-religious experiences in the laboratory. Joseph Smith and other religious visionaries were probably frauds, they say, but may have also been afflicted by temporal lobe epilepsy.[15] Because visions can be replicated by altering neurological conditions, says the atheist, it's clear that all spiritual experiences are only in someone's head.

---

14 See, for instance, Dawkins's attempt to refute "The argument from personal experience," in *The God Delusion*, 112–15.

15 There's no evidence that Joseph Smith or any other major religious figure of history had temporal lobe epilepsy, but, in the circular logic of the atheist, they *must* have had the condition or else what's the explanation for their experiences?

RESPONSES TO MATERIALISTS

To respond to these dismissals of religious experiences, it's first important to note that the similarities between spiritual experiences and brain manipulations are extremely tenuous. Few hallucinogenic drug users come down from their high claiming that what they saw was real, while those who have had religious visions are adamant that their experiences were far more real than anything in their lives. All those who have felt both the peace of God and the "peace" of chemical sedation know that they are qualitatively different. Multiple returners have also undergone the God Helmet treatment and found that it produced nothing even close to what they experienced in their NDE.

When oxygen-deprived pilots hallucinate seeing loved ones, none claim to have *actually* seen them—they recognize it as a hallucination—but when someone has cardiac arrest and claims to have seen deceased relatives on the other side, they have no doubt that what they experienced was real. They even lose all fear of death. In recounting his own near-death experience, Father Richard John Neuhaus said, echoing prophetic certainty, "It happened—as surely, as simply, as undeniably as it happened that I tied my shoes this morning. I could as well deny the one as deny the other."[16] Experiences of God are, in fact, so real that they have caused convinced atheists (notably A. J. Ayer—one of the most important logical positivists and atheists of the twentieth century) to seriously doubt or completely turn away from their atheism.[17]

And if NDEs are the result of hypoxia (oxygen deprivation), then why have many people with plenty of oxygen experienced NDEs? Conversely, why have so many people without oxygen not experienced an NDE? If medication causes the experiences, then why do we find NDEs among those who are on no medications at all? And if NDEs are a function of brain activity, why do so many have NDEs when their brains are completely shut down?[18]

---

16 Richard John Neuhaus, *As I Lay Dying* (NY: Basic Books, 2003), 114.

17 A. J. Ayer, "What I Saw When I Was Dead," 1988, accessed May 31, 2016, available at www.philosopher.eu/others-writings/a-j-ayer-what-i-saw-when-i-was-dead/.

18 Ring, *Lessons from the Light*; and Van Lommel, *Consciousness Beyond Life*.

Returners also report on matters they couldn't have known were they just hallucinating. Many relate details of the operation that would not have been available from inside their bodies. Some witness actions or conversations in another room, later verified by others; some meet people on the other side who they don't recognize, only later to find out, via photographs, that they were deceased relatives; and others even report seeing objects on the roof of the hospital that are later recovered. Brain science is completely inadequate to explain this.[19]

Not only are returners adamant that their experiences were real and much different from a hallucination, but they also experience significant life changes. People come back from their NDEs and are more loving, compassionate, concerned for others, and less materialistic. Compare that to the drug user who is ever-more pathological after his chemically induced highs.

If there were, in fact, an afterlife, then we would expect it to be as returners describe it: peace and love in God's presence. But if NDEs were the product of oxygen deprivation or brain malfunction, we would expect them to be random, bizarre, and even grotesque hallucinations, like those experienced by drug users or God Helmet patients.

Darwinian fundamentalists are also confronted with this unanswerable question: what possible evolutionary advantage could there be to an NDE? They tell us that many of our experiences are illusions wired into us by evolution because they have "survival value," yet what survival value would there be to having a pleasant hallucination before dying? Why would evolution "trick us" into seeing these things? Only some extremely creative storytelling could begin to provide an answer.

The much-heralded creation of religious experiences via the God Helmet has also turned out to be mostly groundless. So far, all attempts to duplicate the experiment (a core criterion of scientific validity) have failed. One journalist investigating the God Helmet was puzzled at how little the hallucinations it gave her resembled her previous religious experiences. The attending scientist, she noted, was also quite manipulative. When she reported a lack of spiritual experience under the influence of the God Helmet the scientist became annoyed and used leading questions to get her to say that her experience was more profound and "spiritual"

---

19   Ring, *Lessons from the Light*; and Van Lommel, *Consciousness Beyond Life*.

than it was.[20] In other words, the "scientist" was doing a very unscientific thing—trying to change the data to fit a theory instead of vice versa.

All of this shows that atheists are not nearly as wedded to empiricism as they claim. They say that seeing is believing, but if they saw God or an angel today they would almost certainly maintain that it was simply their brain playing a trick on them. After all, that's what they do with the testimonies of thousands who actually *have* seen God or angels. If seeing is believing for the atheist, then why do they explain away the many sightings of God that real people have had? The atheist claim that seeing is believing is manifestly not true.

But the most fundamental flaw in atheist attempts to explain away religious experiences is that they undercut materialist-empiricism itself. If we can dismiss spiritual experiences (such as feeling the Spirit) by appealing to brain chemistry, we can also dismiss *empirical experiences* in the same way and for the same reasons, thereby rendering science impossible.

Atheists point out that we can replicate some aspects of spiritual experiences by altering the brain, but *we can also replicate aspects of sensory experiences* by altering the brain. Does that explain them away too? If, as the atheist suggests, the reality of an experience is negated by our ability to artificially mimic it, then that would negate *all* human experience, including the scientific or empirical ones.

For example, if we can claim that a returner didn't really see heaven but only *thought* she did because brain manipulation can create an illusion of heaven, then we can also claim that a scientist didn't really see her laboratory but only *thought* she did because brain manipulation can create an illusion of the laboratory. If God isn't real because we can hallucinate Him, then doesn't it follow that your mother also isn't real because we can hallucinate her?

In other words, claiming that religious experiences are false because we can replicate them would logically defeat all other experiences, including scientific observations, because those can be reproduced as well. Too many atheists fail to realize that the existence of something is totally independent of one's illusions about that thing.

Atheists also try to discount spiritual experiences using brain-imaging technology. They say we can reduce religion to brain activity because we

20   Barbara Bradley Hagerty, *Fingerprints of God: What Science Is Learning About the Brain and Spiritual Experience* (NY: Penguin, 2010).

can detect predictable patterns of neurons firing during spiritual experiences. But we can also detect predictable patterns of neurons firing during scientific inquiry, so does that mean science is not real? Why do we get to arbitrarily disqualify spiritual experiences as brain chemistry but not scientific experiences? There is no reason other than prejudice—a dogmatic commitment to materialism. The sad reality is that atheist scientists won't believe in visions, near-death experiences, spiritual manifestations, or revelations, regardless of the thousands of testimonies of their reality, simply because they won't believe anything that doesn't fit into their dogmatic materialist worldview. Seeing is not believing—not even for them.

In this, the atheists behave a little like political ideologues. Liberals and conservatives alike give people on "their side" a pass for some action, but then criticize the same action as intolerable when done by those on the "other side."[21] This kind of double standard is expected in politics—the realm of the tribal, emotional, and irrational—but should have no place in science where we are supposed to submit to facts. Alas, atheist scientists can be just as dogmatic and prejudiced as the political ideologues or religious fanatics they mock.

The scientific method requires that we 1) gather data, 2) develop a theory to explain the data, and 3) test the theory's predictions to either corroborate or falsify the theory. Contrast this to the behavior of atheists who adhere to a unfalsifiable materialist paradigm and, when confronted with evidence to the contrary, explain it away by concocting explanations *ex post* (after the fact). In this, they are acting more like astrologers than scientists, and their attempts to debunk religion end up debunking science as well.

GOD GENE

Nowhere is this tendency more apparent than in the recent explaining away of God using genetics. Some scientists have recently claimed, to great journalistic fanfare, that they have identified a "God gene," meaning

---

21 For instance, it's common for Republicans to criticize President Obama's expansions of federal government power but to remain silent about President Bush's even more extensive expansions. It's common for Democrats to call Republicans "Fascists" but then claim that it's beyond the pale for Republicans to call Democrats "Commies" (and vice versa). It's common for Republicans to criticize large budget deficits when Democrats are in office but to go silent on the matter once Republicans take charge.

that our belief in God is not rooted in reality but in a genetic predisposition.[22] According to *Atlantic* writer Paul Bloom, "Religion emerged not to serve a purpose but by accident."[23] Similarly, Daniel Dennett said that religion is merely a "natural phenomenon."[24]

This is a fascinating and odd position for an atheist to take since it invalidates not just religious knowledge but *all* knowledge. Darwinian fundamentalism tells us that *all* beliefs are the result of evolution-produced genetics, including science, so if a genetic disposition to believe something falsifies it, then science itself has been falsified. Obviously, we get nowhere by trying to "explain away" a belief by appealing to genetics.

For instance, many neuroscientists are political progressives who passionately opposed the Vietnam War, yet numerous studies have shown that genes predispose people to their political ideologies. Does this mean opposing the Vietnam War was incorrect? Hardly. Whether the war was just or unjust is entirely independent of one's genetics. If it was wrong, then a predisposition to believe it was wrong doesn't change its wrongness. Since the truth or falsity of a proposition is independent of whether genetics "program" us to believe it, then the existence of a God gene is totally irrelevant to the question of whether God exists. A science gene wouldn't invalidate science, and a God gene doesn't invalidate God.[25]

Note also the circular and redundant (tautological) nature of the God gene claims. Darwin's theory, at its most basic, says that things came to be

---

22 You find this position in, for example, Matthew Alper, *The "God" Part of the Brain* (Naperville, IL: Sourcebooks, 2008); Dean Hamer, *The God Gene* (NY: Anchor, 2005); John C. Wathey, *The Illusion of God's Presence* (Amherst, NY: Prometheus, 2016); and Heather Horn, "Where does Religion Come From?" *The Atlantic*, August 17, 2011, accessed April 21, 2016, www.theatlantic.com /entertainment/archive/2011/08/where-does-religion-come-from/243723/.

23 Paul Bloom, "Is God an Accident?" *The Atlantic*, December 2005, 105–12.

24 Dennett, *Breaking the Spell*, 24–28, 97–107.

25 Actually, announcing the discovery of the much-hailed God gene was premature. Further investigation has shown that there is no single God gene or science gene or conservative gene or gay gene or any other single gene to explain beliefs, inclinations, and behaviors. Rather, our biological traits emerge from a complex interaction of many genes, not single ones.

as they are because of a series of accidents, and certain accidents (favorable genetic mutations) happen to confer survival value upon the organism which, in turn, passes this trait on to its genetic descendants. In this view, it is by accident that *all* human behaviors and beliefs come to be. How, then, could there *not* be a God gene? To claim that anything (including religious belief or scientific belief) was *not* an accident would be to claim that there was purpose involved (God). Good Darwinian fundamentalists reject purpose out of hand. When they claim that religious belief came about through evolutionary processes, atheists simply repeat what they claim about everything, including science. It's difficult for believers to understand how this tautology of Darwinian fundamentalism is worthy of being reported in the news at the highest levels, but perhaps next month *The Atlantic* will run a cover story breaking the "news" that scientific belief is the result of an evolutionary "accident."

USEFUL LIES

In making the God gene claim, atheists have also set up for themselves the impossible task of explaining why religion, if it were so obviously an illusion, survived genetically over millions of years. The vast majority of people throughout history have believed in deity, so if there were no God, why would evolution trick us into thinking there was?

The answer for Darwinian fundamentalism is that evolution doesn't select for truth, but only for *survival*. Evolution rewards behavior alone, not thought. It doesn't care whether a belief is true; it only cares if it helps humans survive. So religious belief (again, notice the circular reasoning) must have helped our ancestors survive. That is, evolution has wired humans to believe in useful lies, including the existence of God.

Once again, the atheist has completely undercut his own position. If evolution is so powerful that it tricks us into believing useful lies, then on what grounds should we believe in the findings of science? Didn't our ability to do science evolve and isn't science itself, then, also just a useful lie? If we can't trust our experiences because of evolution's omnipotent power to deceive, then why can't we dismiss scientific theories as useful deceptions, including Darwinism itself?

The atheist might counter that we actually *can* trust Darwinism as true because the truth *is* useful. But notice how they've now reversed course. One moment atheists pontificate on evolution's marvelous power to deceive us with useful lies; then in the next moment they say that evolution wouldn't deceive us because lies are not useful. Which is it?

Biologists have long pointed out that we evolved to be afraid of snakes because snakes can be dangerous. This fear helped our ancestors avoid snakes and thus survive to procreate. Our evolved fear of snakes is evidence that evolution selects for truth—snakes and their venom are real after all.

But aren't we also afraid of ghosts, the devil, and divine punishment? If evolution selects for truth, then shouldn't we conclude that ghosts, the devil, and God are real too? Either evolution selects for truth—in which case we can trust religious experiences as true—or evolution selects for usefulness—in which case we can throw out all knowledge, including scientific findings, as useful lies. You cannot have it both ways.

This is the Achilles' heel of Darwinian fundamentalism. The "truth" of the Darwinian view of science is called into doubt once we see everything (including the theory of Darwinism itself), as a survival strategy. The explaining away of belief that atheists engage in destroys the very foundation of atheism. Materialism, it would appear, can't even survive itself.[26]

SO MUCH ILLUSION

At this point, it is worth considering how often atheists appeal to illusion to explain everything that doesn't fit into their materialist-empiricist paradigm. Much, if not most, of what we think, feel, or believe, they say, is actually an evolution-contrived trick. In the words of psychologist Steven Pinker, "Right and wrong, merit and worthlessness, beauty and ugliness, holiness and baseness . . . are neural constructs, movies we project onto the interior of our skulls, ways to tickle the pleasure centers of the brain"; they have "no reality."[27]

You think you feel compassion for strangers, but it's really just your selfish genes engaging in rational survival strategies in the hope of reciprocal altruism. You think you have spiritual experiences, but they are just

---

26   Christian philosopher Alvin Plantinga made a related argument in much more sophisticated and technical form in his book, *Where the Conflict Really Lies: Science, Religion, and Naturalism* (NY: Oxford University Press, 2011).

27   Steven Pinker, *The Blank Slate* (NY: Penguin, 2003), 192.

feelings created by your brain. You think you have free will, but it is a
useful illusion to give the appearance that you are in control of your destiny. You think your life has meaning, but this is an illusion foisted on
you by genes to make you engage in gene-perpetuating activities.[28] You
think you have a mind, but consciousness itself is an illusion. You think
nature has a design, but this also is an illusion—the most intricate objects
imaginable are not really created with purpose but came about by chance.
You think you love the beauty and sublimity of art and nature, but (in an
explanation as convoluted as any conspiracy theory) this is actually a trick
your genes play that also somehow helps you survive.[29] You even think
that you exist as a "self," but that also is an illusion.

Even love for one's own children is merely an illusion. Our selfish
genes want to multiply and spread, so they have created in us the illusion
of love so we will protect those genes that our children carry by watching out for and nurturing them. However, I must wonder how seriously
atheists themselves take this idea. Do atheists, when tucking in their kids
at night, say "I love you," or do they say, "My genes want to perpetuate
themselves through you"?

The atheist view that the fundamental facts of our existence are illusory is well summed up by philosopher Thomas Metzinger: "Thinking
isn't something you do, it's something that happens to you. The self is
a myth. The epistemic subject is a myth. Choice is a myth. They are all
part of the grand Myth of Cognitive Agency which says that we're mentally autonomous beings. We can now see that this is an old complacent
fairy tale."[30]

The materialist view leads to this: Consciousness is an illusion. Choice
is an illusion. Your own existence as a "self" is an illusion. Responsibility
is an illusion. Guilt is an illusion. Meaning is an illusion. Purpose is an
illusion. Moral truth is an illusion. Design is an illusion. Spiritual experience is an illusion. God is an illusion. Love is an illusion.

For a philosophy that claims so stridently to be based in reality,
empiricist-materialism certainly asks us to accept a lot of reality denying.

---

28   Steven Pinker, *The Blank Slate* (NY: Penguin, 2003), 192–93.

29   Multiple atheist scientists make the case for each of these being an illusion in
     Brockman, ed., *This Idea Must Die.*

30   Thomas Metzinger, "Cognitive Agency," in *This Idea Must Die*, 149.

Atheists tell us those things in life we are *most* certain of are all evolution-generated tricks. If Christians invoked illusion as much as the materialists do, they would be ridiculed as superstitious dopes. That atheists can get away with explaining away everything they don't like as illusion and still be referred to as hard-nosed realists shows the degree to which our society's reverence for science has turned cultish and silly.

Once again, atheists are condemned by their own maxim, "extraordinary claims require extraordinary evidence" by making the extraordinary claim that those things we are most certain of are just illusions. Rather than providing extraordinary evidence for this extraordinary claim, they provide none at all. The dogma of materialism is the only basis for all of their illusion talk so they stand condemned by their own criterion.

In Charles Dickens's classic novel *A Christmas Carol*, Marley's ghost appears to Scrooge, engages him in conversation, but then perceives that Scrooge isn't taking him seriously. An interesting exchange follows:

GHOST: You don't believe in me.
SCROOGE: I don't.
GHOST: What evidence would you have of my reality, beyond that of your senses?
SCROOGE: I don't know.
GHOST: Why do you doubt your senses?
SCROOGE: Because a little thing affects them. A slight disorder of the stomach makes them cheats. You may be an undigested bit of beef, a blot of mustard, a crumb of cheese, a fragment of an underdone potato. There's more of gravy than of grave about you, whatever you are![31]

Many of today's atheists echo Scrooge in their preposterous attempts to dismiss evidence as illusory when it doesn't fit their preconceptions. For atheists, seeing is believing until they don't like what they see, at which point they just call it illusion and go on their merry way.

THE COMPANY THEY KEEP

All of this illusion talk also puts atheists in some interesting company. Mary Baker Eddy, the founder of Christian Science, taught that matter, sin, and sickness are not real but only illusions God has given that

---

31   Charles Dickens, *A Christmas Carol* (London: William Heinemann, 1906), 19.

we must learn to overcome.[32] Idealist philosopher and Anglican bishop George Berkeley also denied the reality of the external world, saying that everything we perceive (trees, rocks, soil, mountains, houses, buildings, animals) only exists in the mind of observers. There is no material, he said, only mind. Matter, then, is an illusion created by minds, particularly God's mind.

The Darwinian fundamentalists try to convince us of the same, only replacing "God" with "selfish genes." The fundamental elements of our reality—consciousness, love, meaning, morals, agency, and so forth—are evolution-generated illusions, they say. Is the Darwinian fundamentalist view in which the most basic elements of life are merely tricks played by selfish genes any more credible than Berkeleyan idealism? I don't believe the atheists for the same reason I don't believe Berkeley—both ask me to deny the self-evident realities of which I am most certain. I am more sure of my love for my children than I am of the latest claims of genetic science, so why deny this love as unreal based on the dubious interpretations of certain scientific findings, which, unlike my love for my children, are subject to change, falsification, and reversal?

Many have ridiculed Berkeley's attempt to reduce matter to mind, but is it any more incredible than the atheist attempt to reduce mind to matter? Few take Berkeley's idealism seriously anymore (literary critic Samuel Johnson famously refuted it by kicking a podium). But oddly, people still take seriously the equally implausible illusionism of today's atheists. Common sense suggests that we should reject both materialism and immaterialism as untenable.[33]

---

32 See Mary Baker Eddy, *Science and Health with Key to the Scriptures* (Boston: Christian Science Publishing Society, 1934).

33 Berkeley asked us to take a leap of faith to believe his idealism, but the atheist wants us to take a more incredible leap of faith to believe that accident (or "non-intelligence"), if given enough time, is more intelligent than intelligence. The brain is more magnificent than any man-made computer; the body is a more efficient manufacturing system than any factory; leather is still superior to all the synthetics humans have devised; DNA is in some ways the most ingenious computer code there is; and yet the atheist wants us to believe that the highest achievements of purposeful actors (humans) can't approach the intricacy, perfection, and wonder of mere chance. Believing that requires quite a leap of faith as well.

Atheists often mock the credulity of those who believe God placed evidence for evolution in the fossil record in order to trick us and thereby test our faith. But aren't atheists being equally credulous when they claim that selfish genes trick us with illusions of consciousness, free will, religious experiences, and God?[34] Invoking trickster genes to explain away anything that doesn't fit the empiricist-materialist dogma is hardly an acceptable way for scientists to approach reality. We might expect talk of a higher power playing tricks on us from certain religious fundamentalists, but we should expect better from scientists.

To cling to materialism, then, atheists must take a leap of faith. They want so badly to believe in their unsupported materialism that they are willing to accept the fantastic idea that brain chemistry (for no apparent reason) tricks us into seeing, feeling, and experiencing things that aren't real. That's quite a leap, and yet atheists generally congratulate themselves on being no-nonsense realists.

Latter-day Saints, on the other hand, choose to take spiritual experiences at face value. It may seem hard to believe in miracles, visions, heavenly visitations, and golden plates, but it is much harder to believe that the self, free will, consciousness, love, value, and spiritual experiences are mere illusions. Every human being must take a faith leap of some kind, and the religious leap is far more plausible than the atheist one.

WE DON'T SEE HIM?

Atheists have no choice but to go to these lengths to dismiss religious experiences because they get to the heart of atheism's central argument against God: *we don't see Him.* We know that chairs, buildings, cars, rivers, and canyons exist because we can see them, but since we don't see God, says the atheist, He must not exist. Why would the most important and powerful being in the universe hide Himself from us? This is among the strongest arguments against the existence of God in the atheist arsenal, but it is also found wanting, and LDS theology is more than equipped to deal with it.

First, as we saw above, millions of people throughout history *have* seen God. The atheist (or even theological) claim that nobody sees God

---

34   David Stove, *Darwinian Fairytales* (NY: Encounter, 2007).

just isn't true.[35] Although we don't see Him in the predictable, repeatable ways of science, that doesn't mean He's not seen at all. God does not make himself commonly visible to all people since such perfect knowledge would bring responsibility and condemnation upon us: "For of him unto whom much is given much is required; and he who sins against the greater light shall receive the greater condemnation" (D&C 82:3). It should not surprise us that God leaves us unconstrained when it comes to the choice to believe in Him. Empirical evidence would amount to a kind of force, which would destroy the possibility of faith—the development of which is a primary purpose of mortal life.[36] We only see God after a trial of our faith—a test—but many people have passed that test and have, empirically, seen Him.

Second, even those who have not yet seen God expect to see Him in the future. Latter-day Saints and other Christians believe in a Resurrection in which all will stand before God and, if worthy, live with Him eternally. D&C 93:1 teaches, "It shall come to pass that every soul who forsaketh his sins and cometh unto me, and calleth on my name, and obeyeth my voice, and keepeth my commandments, *shall see my face and know that I am*" (emphasis added).

A few privileged and spiritually advanced souls have seen God in this life, but those who don't can have the assurance of seeing God in the hereafter. The prophet Job expressed this hope, saying, "In my flesh shall I see God" (Job 19:26).[37]

Of course, scientists themselves acknowledge there are plenty of unseen realities that we know exist because of their effects. We don't see a magnetic field, but we do observe its impact on metal. We don't see dark matter, but we do observe its impact on the behavior of astronomical objects. Many of us don't see God, but we do observe His impact on our lives. In this sense, it's no more unscientific to believe in God than it is to believe in a magnetic field or the (usually) invisible air we breathe.

---

35   For the Christian argument that God is invisible, see Michael Novak, *No One Sees God* (NY: Doubleday, 2008).

36   Teryl Givens, *The Crucible of Doubt* (SLC: Deseret Book, 2014).

37   Also see D&C 38:8: "But the day soon cometh that ye shall see me, and know that I am; for the veil of darkness shall soon be rent, and he that is not purified shall not abide the day."

Third, it's not just that we anticipate seeing God one day, but Latter-day Saints also believe that we already *have* seen him in premortality. God will not only be visible to us in the future; He already has been visible to us in the past. One of the more unique Mormon beliefs is that humans had a pre-life just as we will have an afterlife. We lived with God, we knew Christ, and we chose His plan, which included being away from Him for a time. Atheists rail against an invisible God, but they accepted a plan in the premortal world that entailed exactly that.

Although the idea of premortality may not be common among mainstream religions today, the ancient Greeks taught it. Plato actually had a clever argument for a premortal existence. He pointed out that we are born with innate knowledge that didn't come from the senses. For instance, no human has ever seen a true circle. We have seen approximations of circles, but when measured precisely, none is a true, perfect circle. So how do we know what a perfect circle is? Where did this knowledge come from? Plato said we must have carried it with us from a prior existence.[38]

But if we had a premortality, says the atheist, why don't we remember it? The idea that we have a veil drawn over our minds to make us forget premortal consciousness sounds a little too convenient and contrived. Isn't the whole idea of unremembered consciousness just a lame attempt to save the false concept of premortality?

Actually, unremembered consciousness is extremely common. It is characteristic of both infancy and dreams. Humans are conscious and somewhat rational before the age of four, and yet, in our memories, it's as if those years never happened. Our infancy has a "veil" drawn around it. We can watch video of ourselves as toddlers talking, acting, and thinking, yet we have no memory of those events. A whole existence is lost to us. My three-year-old son will remember nothing of his life right now. He and I tell jokes, play games, read stories, watch movies, and even have rational conversations, but as an adult he will have no recollection of any of this. Our current consciousness did not emerge out of nothingness, as materialists say, but out of a previous consciousness that we have no recollection of. If there is a veil around the consciousness we had before the age of

---

38 Noam Chomsky's linguistic theories suggest that these essential categories come hardwired into the brain as a "Universal Grammar" and Chomsky himself has pointed out that there is no visible Darwinian means by which these categories could have evolved through natural selection. See Tom Wolfe, *The Kingdom of Speech* (NY: Little, Brown, and Co., 2016).

four, why is it incredible to say there is a veil around the consciousness we had before birth?

Similarly, we are conscious when dreaming but seldom remember those dreams. How often are we ignorant of the previous night's dreams until something during the day jars our memory of them? And just as our premortal knowledge comes back to us in flashes, so our forgotten dreams are often remembered later as something stimulates the memory. The idea of previous consciousness without remembrance is not so laughable after all; it is quite common.

CONCLUSION

Materialist-empiricism is weak, but the incentives to hold this worldview are strong. Atheists like the totalizing explanation of reality it offers. It lets them off the hook for having to approach the world in all of its wonder, complexity, plurality, and openness. Science is the realm of the precise, the objective, the quantifiable; humanity is the realm of the imprecise, the subjective, and the unquantifiable. Since the human realm is far trickier to understand, many atheists just deny its existence by reducing the human realm to the scientific, thereby eliminating all of that pesky imprecision and subjectivity of humanity. Materialism is a soothing dogma that allows closure and finality on fundamental questions, but it is hardly justified by the evidence.

Chapter 6

THE WAR BETWEEN SCIENCE AND RELIGION

MOST OF US HAVE HEARD all about the war between science and religion. This war, we are told, has played out over the centuries as the forces of reason (science) have battled the forces of superstition (religion). The war supposedly continues today in debates over embryonic stem cell research, the teaching of evolution in schools, and arguments over climate change policy. For all of the sound and fury coming from certain quarters, the reality is that this war is a fiction dreamt up by those who understand neither science nor religion. It comes from the ignorance and arrogance characteristic of fundamentalists on both sides.[1]

On the one hand, misguided scientists dismiss all nonempirical claims to knowledge as delusional. On the other hand, misguided religious believers dismiss all non-revelatory claims to knowledge as delusional. While the scientific fundamentalist says that science invalidates religious knowledge, the religious fundamentalist might say that religion invalidates scientific knowledge.

Both are wrong and guilty of a form of epistemological imperialism—an attempt to impose a single way of knowing on all other fields. In the Middle Ages, religious imperialism seemed to have the upper hand as cultural leaders discounted science for not conforming to religion. Today

---

1   Dawkins demonstrates this ignorance in chapter 8 of *The God Delusion* as does Harris on pages 15–16 of *The End of Faith*. For more on the misperception of the war, see Julie Beck interview with Matt Kaplan, *The Atlantic Online*, October 30, 2015, accessed July 5, 2016, www.theatlantic.com/science/archive/2015/10 /where-magic-meets-science/413317/.

it seems as if scientific imperialism has the upper hand as cultural leaders discount religion for not conforming to science.[2]

The root of such epistemological imperialism is the same as the root of political imperialism: pride. In international affairs, we realize that imperialism—one group conquering another in the name of innate superiority—is immoral and unworkable. But in the world of knowledge, when science tries to conquer religion, too many see such imperialism as "enlightened" and "progressive."[3] Worse still, scientific imperialism is highly unscientific. True science means falsifying our paradigms in the face of contrary evidence; scientific imperialism crams all domains into a scientific framework whether they fit or not.

Far better than scientific or religious imperialism is the gospel perspective, which advocates epistemological *pluralism*. Because Latter-day Saints accept the legitimacy of both study (science) and faith (revelation), we are not stuck in the false paradigm of a science-religion war. We understand that these two routes to knowledge are not opposed but complementary.

The gospel emphasizes the science-religion harmony better than perhaps any other faith tradition. LDS prophets and scriptures have long taught that all truth, from whatever source, is part of one great whole. When Henry Eyring, Sr., one of the great scientists of the twentieth century, left home to study at the University of Arizona his father told him, "In this church you don't have to believe anything that isn't true. You go over to the University of Arizona and learn everything you can, and whatever is true is a part of the gospel."[4]

Sociological data supports this harmony of LDS religion with science. There are more scientists per capita among Mormons than any other religion, and religiosity among Latter-day Saints increases with science

---

2   Economist Friedrich Hayek referred to scientific imperialism as scientism—the false belief that science is an exclusive and universal means to knowledge.

3   For an example of the scientific imperialism perspective, see Dennett, *Breaking the Spell*, chapter 2.

4   Henry Eyring, "My Father's Formula," *Ensign*, November 1978, accessed June 24, 2016, available at www.lds.org/ensign/1978/10/my-fathers-formula?lang=eng.

education while, in most other faiths, it declines.[5] Mormons accept both science and religion and realize that, properly understood, there is no contradiction between the two.

In seeking truth, which, by definition, is God's truth, scientists are engaged in godly work. Elder Boyd K. Packer even spoke of truth-pursuing scientists as being "inspired."[6] Previous generations of scientists recognized this. After discovering the laws of planetary motion, Johannes Kepler fell to his knees and thanked God for revealing himself to a humble servant. Isaac Newton, the greatest scientist in history, dedicated half of his life to science but (embarrassingly for current-day materialists) dedicated the other half of his life to theology.[7] Virtually all of the truly great scientists throughout history were religious believers, including Aristotle, Galileo, Boyle, Franklin, Planck, Heisenberg, Einstein, and even (for most of his life) Darwin. Some of them, such as Copernicus, Lemaître, and Mendel, were even clergymen. One of the world's great physicists, Freeman Dyson of Princeton's Institute for Advanced Study, is not only a Christian but holds Latter-day Saints in high esteem. A recent *New York Times* interviewer asked him, "What books might we be surprised to find on your shelves?" Dyson answered, "The Book of Mormon: Another Testament of Jesus Christ. I treasure it because some of my best friends are Mormons, and the book tells a dramatic story in a fine biblical style. The reader has to wait with growing tension almost until the end of the story

---

5   Stan L. Albrecht, "The Consequential Dimension of Mormon Religiosity," in *Latter-Day Saint Social Life, Social Research on the LDS Church and its Members* (Provo, Utah: BYU Religious Studies Center, 1998), 286.

6   Boyd K. Packer, "The Light of Christ," *Ensign*, April 2005; and Boyd K. Packer, "Revelation in a Changing World," *Ensign*, November 1989.

7   In fact, science itself has shown the weakness of scientific imperialism. Philip Tetlock, in an extensive study of the greatest test of intellectual accuracy—forecasting—showed that those who attempt to stuff all knowledge into a single model (Hedgehogs) are far less effective in arriving at truth than those willing to use a variety of models (Foxes). The intellectual pluralism of the gospel, these studies suggest, is far preferable to the intellectual imperialism of the atheists. Philip Tetlock, *Expert Political Judgment* (Princeton: Princeton University Press, 2006); and Philip E. Tetlock and Dan Gardner, *Superforecasting* (NY: Crown, 2015).

to reach the final climax, when Jesus arrives in America and founds his second kingdom here."[8]

Sociologist Rodney Stark has argued that far from having an adversarial relationship, Christianity and science have had a symbiotic one. Science grew out of Christianity's belief in a universal, reasonable God who gave us intelligence such that we could discover His workings and thereby glorify Him.[9] Contrary to what some fundamentalists on both sides might say, there is nothing intrinsically atheistic about science and, in fact, we find a deep harmony and complementarity between science and religion.

GOD OF THE GAPS

Nevertheless, under the paradigm of a science-religion war, the fundamentalists believe that, as on a battlefield, an advance by one side means a retreat by the other. This leads to a "God of the gaps" religious view. To the atheist, religious believers cling to their belief in God by pointing to something that science hasn't yet explained (a gap) and then, once science explains it, retreating to a narrower gap. God, atheists charge, is just a name for what science has yet to discover and with each new scientific advance religion retreats a little more.[10]

Atheists are right to criticize the God of the gaps, for such a god is not a very worthy god at all. If we peg our faith to gaps in scientific knowledge, then our faith must get ever smaller as the domain of science gets ever larger. With the God of the gaps, a gain for science is indeed a loss for faith.

But Latter-day Saints are not forced to believe in a God of the gaps because our God is not found in what science has *not yet* explained but rather in 1) the findings of science itself (science reveals God's truth after all) and 2) what science *cannot* explain. Some matters are not gaps in

---

8   Freeman Dyson, "By The Book," *New York Times, Sunday Book Review*, April 16, 2015, accessed July 13, 2016, www.nytimes.com/2015/04/19/books /review/19bkr-bythebook_dyson.t.html?. Dyson once told me in conversation that his greatest contribution to Christianity is his daughter, a Christian minister.

9   Rodney Stark, *For the Glory of God* (Princeton: Princeton University Press, 2004). For more on this and a debunking of the simplistic "war" between science and religion, see Ronald L. Numbers, ed., *Galileo Goes to Jail and Other Myths about Science and Religion* (Cambridge: Harvard University Press, 2010).

10   Dawkins, *The God Delusion*, 151–55.

science but are beyond the ken of science all together. Science is incapable of answering myriad questions. In other words, we may not believe in a God of the gaps, but there is a great case to be made for a "God of the limits."

For instance, atheists often say that with time we'll be able to explain consciousness in material terms. This is an example of what philosopher Karl Popper called promissory materialism. Popper noted that for centuries, materialists have been saying, "Our discovery of a material basis for consciousness is right around the corner." However, this discovery is never forthcoming.[11] We are still waiting, and we will remain waiting forever because consciousness is, by its nature, nonmaterial and cannot be observed empirically. It falls outside the scientific purview. Saying that we will someday find a material basis for consciousness is like saying we will someday find a square circle. It's impossible. Consciousness is a limit to science, not a gap.

Scientists examine that which is regular, predictable, and repeatable, but many of the most profound and revealing experiences of our lives are not regular, predictable, or repeatable. If someone sees a vision or has an intuition of a future event and then sees that future come to pass, the experience clearly gave them knowledge. Such experiences are not scientific, but to say that this discounts their reality is unjustified and arrogant. Religion's war, then, is not with science but with a scientific imperialism that has nothing to do with true science.

DON'T SCIENTISTS TEND ATHEIST?

If there is no war between science and religion, why do we find that many scientists, including the most visible ones (such as Stephen Hawking, Carl Sagan, Richard Dawkins, Neil deGrasse Tyson, and Bill Nye), are outspoken atheists? If science and religion are so compatible, why does it seem like the scientific community as a whole is hostile to religion?

Actually, the scientific community is not nearly as atheistic as many of its self-proclaimed spokesmen would have us believe. Surveys report that about 50 percent of scientists believe in God or a higher power, and this number has not changed in over a century. There has hardly been a mass retreat from religion among scientists.[12]

---

11   Karl Popper and John Eccles, *The Self and Its Brain* (London: Routledge, 1977).

12   Paul Bloom, "Is God an Accident?" *The Atlantic*.

The stereotype that science and atheism go together may persist largely because our sensationalist media gives special attention to the most strident voices for any political, cultural, or economic viewpoint. Naturally, the most combative and outspoken of scientists are held up by the media as representatives of the scientific community, so the public comes to associate the typical scientist with someone like Dawkins. In reality, zealous antireligion scientists are an embarrassment to many of their colleagues and hardly represent the norm among scientists generally. However, the media helps create the false appearance that there is an anti-religion scientific consensus. Most religious believers reject antiscience fundamentalism and most scientists reject antireligious fundamentalism, yet this reality is obscured because we treat the most contentious voices on both sides as somehow representative of the entire group.

REASONS FOR SCIENTIFIC IRRELIGIOSITY

While it isn't true that scientists are overwhelmingly atheist, it is true that they are less religious than the public at large. About 80 percent of Americans believe in a personal God, while among scientists it is less than half that.[13] If we must trust scientists as authorities and if scientists are less religious than average, then doesn't this give credence to the atheist point of view? Could materialism really become so dominant among scientists if it wasn't intellectually well-founded? Even if scientists are not as antireligion as the media would make them out to be, doesn't the fact that they are less religious than the public at large support the idea that there is something fundamentally antireligion about science?

These are legitimate questions, but the answer to each is "no." While atheists would have us believe that becoming scientifically enlightened leads one to reject religious superstition, we can actually account for the low religiosity among scientists by looking at sociology and incentives. It's not science itself that leads to irreligion but the *interests and groupthink* of the scientific community.

In every academic field, particular paradigms often take hold for reasons unrelated to that field. In my own field of history, for instance, the paradigm of left wing or progressive politics is even more domi-nant than materialism is in science, yet there is nothing about history

---

13   Paul Bloom, "Is God an Accident?" *The Atlantic.*

that naturally leads to such views.[14] As with the atheism of scientists, the progressive leaning of historians has little to do with the merits of progressive politics and everything to do with self-interest and groupthink (the conservative leanings of wealthy businesspeople can likely be explained the same way).[15]

The Progressive Myth tells the historian that heroes have always been working toward progress (abolitionists, civil rights activists, anti-imperialists, feminists, champions of the poor), and villains have always resisted it (conservatives or reactionaries). Since Thomas Jefferson, Abraham Lincoln, Elizabeth Cady Stanton, Mahatma Gandhi, Martin Luther King, Jr., and other heroes of the past were "on the right side of history," historians then apply the label "progressive" or "liberal"[16] to these individuals and claim them as allies in present-day political battles. Signing up for anything labeled "progressive" in the present then makes the historian a hero in her own narrative and the latest in a long line of champions of justice that includes all of those mentioned above.[17]

---

14   Multiple studies have borne this out. See, for instance, Jon A. Shields and Joshua M. Dunn Sr., *Passing on the Right* (NY: Oxford University Press, 2016); and Scott Jaschik, "Social Scientists Lean to the Left, Study Says," *Inside Higher Ed.*, December 21, 2005, accessed January 31, 2017, available at www.insidehighered.com/news/2005/12/21/politics.

15   This is not a castigation of progressive politics—there are sound reasons to hold certain beliefs of both the left and right—it is only a castigation of how many historians *arrive* at these politics. Both the regnant American ideologies of progressivism and conservatism are incoherent grab bags of political ideas that contain some truth and much falsehood, but the fact that historians buy into the entire package of progressivism tells us much about their inability to carefully reason when a socially created paradigm has taken over their thinking. Those who can have the most subtlety and nuance when discoursing about, say, the complexity of fourteenth-century French peasantry, suddenly have no capacity for nuance when it comes to politics. This dogmatism suggests that historians arrive at their politics through other means than careful reasoning.

16   While I often call myself a liberal in the tradition of John Locke, John Stuart Mill, and Karl Popper, the word has such various meanings in the USA that it's often used as a synonym for "progressive."

17   One finds a funny inconsistency at work among fashionably left-wing atheists who criticize American capitalism on the grounds that it encourages empty materialism, even as their whole philosophy of life is premised on materialism. Material acquisition is the norm in nature, so if people are merely natural beings,

Progressivism also appeals to most historians' financial interests as well since they are usually on the government payroll (working for tax-funded universities and/or receiving government-funded research grants) and stand to benefit financially from increasing the government's scope and spending. The progressive goal of massive state control of society would mean that intellectuals, rather than capitalists, would command society's economic resources. A redistribution of wealth also means a redistribution of power, and intellectuals have much to gain by that redistribution. Given all of this, it should not surprise us that historians favor the public sector at the expense of the private.

All communities, even scholarly ones, are marked by the tendency to adopt the beliefs of peers, even if those beliefs are irrational. The desire to fit in with one's colleagues as one of the good guys working for social justice provides a serious incentive for historians to adopt a certain political point of view. Socialism (even Marxist socialism) is prevalent in history departments, not because it's intellectually valid but because declaring a commitment to socialism has become a way to signal high moral standing to other historians. In order to thrive in the historical profession—for example, appeal to admissions committees, get published, find favor with advisors, win over hiring committees, and be accepted at historical conferences—it helps to adopt the fashionable paradigm of that profession.[18] If groupthink can cause someone to think that a four-inch line is longer than an six-inch line (as the Asch conformity experiments have shown), it can certainly lead otherwise rational historians to accept the absurdities of

how can scientific materialists criticize American materialist consumerism? That scientific materialists oppose economic materialism with a straight face is something I've long found quite amusing.

18 I was once at a roundtable discussion where a distinguished historian from Yale was met with ridicule for praising the American Founders. He attempted to defend himself by saying, "Look, I'm a good liberal like the rest of you." A declaration of political conformity had become a precondition of acceptance in the historical community. Many times, history professors have pulled me behind closed doors to confess a conservative belief (such as opposition to race-based admission policies or the cancelling of western civilization courses), but then asked me to keep their heresies secret lest they be ostracized by their colleagues. Departments on university campuses can be prisons of orthodoxy where conformity to the dominant political paradigm is often a precondition of acceptance and success.

Marxism.[19] Political leftism, in other words, isn't something that historians arrive at after their study of history; it's a peer-provided starting point that frames inquiry and shapes interpretation. It's a faith.[20]

SCIENTIST GROUPTHINK AND INTEREST

Compare this to science. Just as it is in the historian's interest to buy into progressivism, so it is in the scientist's interest to buy into materialist-empiricism. Some scientists might denigrate religion in the name of enhancing their own power: the less people turn to religion for answers to life's questions, the more they turn to science. If scientists can declare everything nonscientific to be illusory, then they have set themselves up as the only legitimate purveyors of knowledge in society. Under materialism, everyone, from the priest to the politician, must bow to the superior wisdom of the scientist, so naturally the scientist has an incentive to promote the materialist philosophy. In religious societies, cultural power is vested in God and the clergy, but if the intellectuals dispense with God, they themselves become a secular clergy—the learned champions of enlightenment against backwardness and superstition.

We understand that a candidate for office wants to damage the credibility of their opponent—a competitor for political power—but scientists have an equal motive for damaging the credibility of religion—it is a competitor for cultural power. Scientists, then, promote atheism for the same reason dictators shoot rivals—it furthers their narrow interest.

Of course, atheists deny that it's in their self-interest to champion materialism. They have created a narrative in which scientists are

19   Recent polls show that there are far more Marxists among historians than Republicans. Rationality can't account for this but groupthink can. See, for instance, Jon A. Shields and Joshua M. Dunn Sr., *Passing on the Right* (NY: Oxford University Press, 2016); and Jonathan Haidt, *The Righteous Mind* (NY: Pantheon, 2012).

20   In fact, many historians have never even considered a contrary point of view. Posing even the simplest rebuttals to leftist orthodoxies leaves some of my history PhD colleagues speechless. It's not that they've considered and then rejected non-leftist points of view, it's that they've never even been exposed to them. Their "progressivism" is often more a function of ignorance than enlightenment. Ironically, the most learned people in society can, by being surrounded by people who think exactly like them, also be the most cloistered and provincial.

courageous dissenters from a religion-dominated culture. They are "free-thinkers" and "brights" (Dawkins's preferred term for atheists), while everyone else is conformist and, presumably, dull. But this self-serving narrative could only work on the level of the culture as a whole and does not take into account the microculture of science itself, which is a much more important force for conformity. A true freethinker would be willing to challenge the dogmas of their immediate peers; atheists are unwilling to do this. Is it really courageous to be a materialist when nearly everyone you associate with daily is also a materialist? That most Americans are not LDS hardly makes a Mormon living in Provo, Utah, a dissenter, and that most Americans are religious hardly makes a materialist scientist in an academic department a dissenter. The freethinking atheists, then, resemble the proverbial thundering herd of independent minds running along with their peer group and priding themselves on their independence while manifesting very little.

Some atheists say that religious people have an authoritarian personality, meaning they are too easily controlled by charismatic religious figures who claim authority from God.[21] These atheists tell themselves that their opponents are like sheep blindly following authority. But the problem of the mindless following of authority is at least as pronounced among atheists as it is among the religious. While it's true that we can explain religiosity by looking at sociology—people are far more likely to be religious when their peer group is—scientists are not immune to this same social pressure.

At some point, the materialist tendency among scientists gathered a self-generating momentum. Once a critical mass of scientists decided that materialism wasn't only a useful scientific assumption but a necessary totalizing worldview, other scientists simply fell in line as a matter of social conformity. New scientists entering the profession naturally wanted to fit in with their academic peers, so they uncritically adopted the dominant materialist paradigm. They hadn't considered or deeply engaged the materialist philosophy (which, as we've seen in previous chapters, is extremely weak); they simply accepted it as what scientists believe. The narrow philosophical assumptions of the scientific community meant that religious believers, like conservatives in history departments, were marginalized

---

21 A claim famously made by Marxists of the Frankfurt School in their book *The Authoritarian Personality* (Oxford: Harpers, 1950).

and ridiculed. Religious scientists didn't go away, but they were banished to the margins or cowed into silence.

It is clear that all communities, including scientific ones, use dogmas to create cohesion, a sense of moral meaning, and perhaps even a sense of superiority. I've learned to distrust the progressivism of my own field as a sociologically created academic fad, and scientists should learn to distrust the materialism of their field for the same reason. Scientists may indeed be less religious than the society at large, but this has less to do with science and more to do with interests and groupthink. Just as some of the most brilliant and truly freethinking historians of the world reject the progressivism dominant in the historical profession,[22] so some of the most brilliant and freethinking scientists in the world have rejected the materialism dominant in the scientific profession. They understand that you can think yourself to more complex positions than the comfortable assumptions that dominate a field. What we call the authority of science against religion is actually just a prejudice created by intellectual imperialists and reinforced by the groupthink and interests of the scientific community.

There is one final (and uncomfortable) element of self-interest that may drive many scientists' tendency to atheism: the simple desire to sin. Humans have always sought to rationalize wrong behaviors, and many of today's intellectuals are no different. If there is no God, then there is no law (see 2 Nephi 2:13). Many atheists openly admit that they don't want there to be a God because He gets in the way of their fun. In a godless world, they have free rein to indulge their carnal inclinations without restraint. They can dismiss any guilt they feel for such behaviors as an outdated vestige of evolution. A godless universe is also a morally relativist one, and this is highly attractive in an age of substance abuse, endless material acquisition, and general hedonism.

People with sound common sense know that there are moral absolutes that we are obliged to obey. Intellectuals, on the other hand, are

---

22 Including Harvard's Niall Ferguson, Brown's Gordon Wood, Penn's Walter McDougall, and Yale's John Lewis Gaddis. Also consider that a central historical lesson of twentieth-century history is the futility of statist socialism as a workable economic model. The histories of Russia, China, Eastern Europe, Cuba, Korea, and Southeast Asia prove definitively that state ownership of economic resources leads to stagnation, poverty, and starvation. Given this overwhelming historical evidence, shouldn't historians be less inclined to socialism? The fact that they are more inclined shows, once again, that their politics likely have little to do with their study of history.

clever enough to find ways to wriggle out of this self-evident truth and thereby open up for themselves all sorts of forbidden behaviors. Common people generally know when they do wrong and admit it; intellectuals justify their wrongdoing by reducing human beings to materials that are answerable to no higher authority. Since they "break the law," "abide not the law," and "altogether abide in sin," they seek to become "a law unto themselves" (D&C 88:35). Those who wish to live a hedonistic lifestyle will also wish for a world without a God who would forbid it. While both believers and atheists sin, believers at least recognize sin and accept the guilt that can lead them to repent. Of the four steps in repentance—recognize, confess, ask forgiveness, and forsake—we usually think of recognition as the easiest. But in our world of moral relativism, most never even make it that far. They rationalize their actions, evade responsibility, and never confront the fact that they are doing anything wrong.

For some reason, as we saw with Korihor (see Alma 30), sexual promiscuity is especially high on the list of sins atheists are eager to commit. It's no coincidence that shortly after writing *The God Delusion*, Richard Dawkins came out in favor of open marriage. And it's no coincidence that Christopher Hitchens wrote *God Is Not Great*, while, at the same time, admitting he didn't like religion because it would forbid him from engaging in "sexual congress" with whomever he wished.[23] Philosopher Bertrand Russell, the leading atheist of the early twentieth century, was not only a prominent opponent of religion but also of sexual fidelity. Atheist Aubrey de Grey is perhaps most candid of all, telling us, "There is nothing about sex that morally distinguishes it from other activities that are performed by two (or more) people collectively. In a world no longer driven by reproductive efficiency, and on the presumption that all parties are taking appropriate precautions in relation to pregnancy and disease, sex is overwhelmingly a recreational activity. What, then, can morally

---

23 See Bertrand Russell, *Autobiography* (NY: Routledge, 1998); Russell, *Why I am Not a Christian* (NY: Routledge, 2004); Russell, *Religion and Science* (NY: Henry Holt, 1935); and Russell, *Marriage and Morals* (NY: Liveright, 1929). See Christopher Hitchens interview with Sam Tanenhaus, May 13, 2007, *The New York Times Book Review podcast*, accessed July 22, 2009, available from www.nytimes.com/ref/books/books-podcast-archive.html. Also see Hitchens interview with Brian Lamb, *C-Span Q&A*, April 26, 2009, accessed July 22, 2009, available from www.q-and-a.org/Program/?ProgramID=1229.

distinguish it from other recreational activities?"[24] We can and should, de Grey concludes, change sex partners as easily and frequently as we do chess partners, lunch partners, workout partners, or video game partners.

Dawkins is equally candid about the inseparability of his antireligious and sexual views. He tells us, "Only a person infected by the sort of sanctimonious self-righteousness that religion uniquely inspires would apply the meaningless word "sin" to private sexual behavior. . . . Why are we so obsessed with monogamous fidelity in the first place. . . . Why should you deny your loved one the pleasure of sexual encounters with others, if he or she is that way inclined?"[25] I suspect that, like Korihor, wanting to engage in illicit sex is a strong motivation for many people becoming atheists in the first place.

The scriptures teach of an intrinsic connection between sexual sin and lack of faith (see D&C 63:16 and 42:23), and while many people have sincere and legitimate questions and doubts, it's also true that sin provides a strong motivation to reject God. Doing away with God is an easy way to sidestep the law of chastity. This could also help us understand why men, more inclined to sins of the flesh, are more likely to be atheists than women. Intellectual reasons for atheism are frequently just a cover for sinful behavior.

We sometimes think that people first identify themselves as atheist and only then conclude they don't have to follow God's restrictions. Actually, it's often the other way around. People first disobey the commandments and then, having driven the Spirit out of their lives and wanting to continue their misdeeds, conclude there is no God. That's probably the more common path to skepticism. For many, it's easier to reject God and thereby deny the need for repentance than it is to actually repent. Faith begins with a desire to believe, and a loss of faith begins with a desire to *dis*believe. It seems that the "Will to Believe" described by philosopher William James[26] has a corollary in the equally strong "Will to Disbelieve" one sees among many atheists.

---

24 Aubrey de Grey, "The Overdue Demise of Monogamy," in *This Explains Everything*, 17.

25 Dawkins, "Banishing the Green-Eyed Monster," *The Washington Post Online*.

26 William James, *The Will to Believe and Other Essays* (NY: Longmans, Green, and Co., 1908).

Recent research has validated this point. Psychologists Jason Weeden and Robert Kurzban distinguish between freewheelers (people more given to promiscuous lifestyles) and ring bearers (those who are more abstemious and save sexuality for marriage) and then show that religiosity is "an effect rather than a cause of" a ring-bearer lifestyle.[27] People don't leave their faith and *then* engage in freewheeling behaviors but rather engage in freewheeling behaviors and *then* leave their faith. This gives empirical support to Cardinal Spellman's oft-quoted aphorism from his popular radio program: "If you don't behave as you believe, you will end up believing as you behave."

Perceptive Latter-day Saints have known this for years. We often see people leaving the Church citing intellectual reasons (uncomfortable facts in Church history, disagreements with Church leaders, the Book of Abraham translation) only to find out later that they carried major sins. Many worthy members have legitimate questions and doubts, but often people lose testimony only after first losing the desire to believe. When they no longer want to believe, they will look for evidence against the gospel and ignore evidence in favor. Some people see the thousands of evidences for the Book of Mormon and say, "This is overwhelming proof that the book is true." Others look at the same evidence and shrug. The difference is faith—the desire to believe. Many atheists, then, don't reject religion because they are "too smart for it" but because they desire to engage in sinful behaviors and desires are at the core of what we choose to believe.

CONCLUSION

The above should make clear that, as with the progressivism of historians, the atheism of scientists is often caused by factors other than knowledge intrinsic to the profession. We are all susceptible to self-interest and groupthink, and scientists are no exception. The power and prestige that comes to scientists who conform to materialism can largely explain their lack of religiosity—not science itself. The more we grow in knowledge and wisdom, the more we realize that the war between science and

---

27   Jason Weeden and Robert Kurzban, *The Hidden Agenda of the Political Mind* (Princeton: Princeton University Press, 2014), 88.

religion always has been and always will be a fiction dreamt up by those who understand neither science nor religion.

Chapter 7

THE GOOD DELUSION

WHILE THE REALITY OF MIND is one proof that materialism is false, the reality of good and evil is another. If, as atheists insist, our belief in God is just a trick played on us by millions of years of evolution, why is it not the same with our belief in good (morality)? If our experiences of God are just feelings that we can ignore, then why aren't our experiences of good also just feelings that we can likewise ignore? "Moral" is simply a name we give to certain behaviors we prefer, but isn't our preference for these behaviors, like our belief in God, just a product of evolution that we can now disregard?

Many atheists want to dispense with the supernaturalism of God and the soul but not the supernaturalism of meaning and morality. They can't have it both ways: a philosophy that dismisses *God* on materialist-empiricist grounds must also dismiss *good* on those same grounds. The "God delusion" necessarily implies the "good delusion."

MORALS ARE NOT EMPIRICAL

Let's begin with the problem of morals and empiricism. Believers have long claimed that religion and morality go hand in hand. For centuries, cultural leaders taught that bolstering religion would also bolster public morals. President George Washington spoke forcefully of the link between morality and religion in his farewell address. Politicians and Supreme Court justices routinely spoke of religious belief as necessary to maintain public trust and virtue. Even most atheists of previous generations thought that we should keep God's nonexistence a secret in order to preserve morality and order in society. They treated religion as a benign illusion—something they couldn't personally accept but thought was generally useful for the masses.

The New Atheists will have none of this. They become angry at the idea that morals depend on God. They claim, with characteristic snark, that we don't need a nonexistent God to tell us what is right and wrong; science can provide us with morals just fine.[1]

This is quite a strange claim coming from staunch empiricists. They are adamant that we can only know what we can see. But when has anyone ever seen morals? Atheists won't believe in God because He is invisible, but they are all too happy to believe in an equally invisible something called "the good." They reject one superstition while clinging tightly to another. Why the double standard? There never has been a scientist who doesn't know what's morally right and consults science to find out. Science only deals in the realm of the empirical, and morals are outside this realm.

An atheist might retort that we can see good in the brain because the brain lights up when someone performs a moral action or has a virtuous thought.[2] However, that is a little like saying we can see a zebra in the brain just because the brain lights up when someone sees a zebra. Neither the zebra nor good is in the brain. It's only neurological activity associated with an experience, but it's decidedly not the *object* of that experience. And if good is real because we can see the brain light up when someone experiences good, does that mean God is real because the brain lights up when someone experiences God (as numerous scientific studies have shown)?[3] This "reality through brain activity" reasoning would dispense quite easily with atheism itself.

A consistent atheist empiricist would realize that we can't see good any more than we can see God, so it can't be any more real. If we cannot

1   See, for instance, Dawkins, *The God Delusion*, chapter 6; Dennett, Breaking the Spell, chapter 10; and Harris, *The End of Faith*, chapter 6.

2   Sam Harris makes this neuroscience case for morality off and on in T*he Moral Landscape.*

3   Jacqueline Howard, "Religious thoughts trigger reward systems like love, drugs," *CNN*, November 29, 2016, accessed January 31, 2017, available at www.cnn .com/2016/11/29/health/religious-brain-mormon-mri/.

believe in what we don't see, then we cannot believe in morality. This moral-empirical problem is an insuperable hurdle for the atheist.

MORALS ARE NOT MATERIAL

Materialism poses as big a challenge to morality as does empiricism. Quite simply, materialism is incompatible with morality because morals are not material. It is neither moral nor immoral for grains of sand to scatter, for air molecules to blow eastward, for a comet to follow a particular orbit, or for a cat to chase a mouse. There is no right or wrong among atoms, molecules, dirt, rocks, comets, planets, or galaxies, so how can it be any different for those purely material entities we call humans? Material is neither good nor evil; it just is.

Let's use the case of murder to illustrate. If humans are mere material, then a murderer is only rearranging matter (the assemblage of atoms we call a human body) in space. The molecules that make up a hill of sand rearrange without moral implication, so why can't the molecules that make up a human body rearrange (what we call death) without moral implication as well?

Our common sense tells us that murder is evil—that it is something *more* than a rearranging of matter—but the atheist can't do so without exiting his materialist framework and assigning some higher, nonmaterial value to the human body. We would probably laugh if someone said it was morally right that oceans consist of saltwater or that a continental plate rearranges matter by drifting northward, yet atheists say it is morally right that other materials (humans) are arranged in a random way and that it's immoral to rearrange them. Materialists can only have morality if they sneak immaterialism in through the back door.

Atheists of previous generations understood this. Bertrand Russell spent the first half of his life in philosophy and the latter half of his life in moral crusades (such as nuclear disarmament), all the while admitting that, as an atheist, he had no way to justify his preferred morals.[4] He said, "I cannot . . . prove that my view of the good life is right; I can only state my view, and hope that as many as possible will agree."[5]

---

4   Russell, *Autobiography.*

5   Russell, *Why I am Not a Christian* (NY: Touchstone, 1957), 56.

Philosopher Friedrich Nietzsche recognized that you can't have your materialist cake and eat it too. If God is dead, then our old concepts of morality are dead too, implying a radical transvaluation of values and movement beyond good and evil. Nietzsche understood something the New Atheists don't: either we live in a materialist universe in which immaterial things such as morals are baseless superstitions or we don't. I urge atheists to be like Nietzsche and stand with the courage of their atheist convictions. If we are, indeed, just material, then they should stop all talk of morality, for it must be a fiction every bit as illusory as God.

MORALS FROM UTILITARIANISM

Because there are no morals in matter, atheists have gotten creative trying to figure out how to preserve good in a godless world. New Atheist Sam Harris has recently written an entire book arguing that we can get morals from science by using "well-being" as our guide.[6] We can know what contributes to human well-being through scientific investigation, says Harris, so science can tell us what we ought to do. For example, certain studies have found that community makes us happy (contributes to our well-being), so communal activity is objectively moral. Likewise, charitable giving contributes to human well-being so it also is objectively moral.[7] We don't need God to know this—we just need the scientific method.

But Harris's quest for a scientific ethics is exposed as futile once we remember the most basic and defining characteristic of science: testability. True science means generating explanatory theories whose value is determined by the theory's ability to predict certain outcomes. If the prediction fails, the theory has been falsified.

What could ever falsify our moral principles? Could Harris ever go into a laboratory and falsify the proposition that compassion is preferable to cruelty? Could we ever find out through science that it's okay to steal, murder, or enslave? Would anyone ever look in a microscope and then pronounce, "I've just found out that it's morally correct to torture innocents"? Can we imagine a student saying, "I only found out it was wrong

---

6   Harris, *Moral Landscape*, 12.

7   Ibid., 2–3.

to murder after taking a course in evolutionary biology"? Because the answer to each is "no," it's clear that science cannot inform morality for moral propositions are unfalsifiable. No atheist scientist is looking to falsify their moral beliefs, and this is all the proof we need that those moral beliefs are not scientific.

Harris's reasoning has three other major problems. First, the idea that we *should* pursue happiness is not itself a scientific proposition. Why couldn't power, pleasure, control, enlightenment, experience, growth, domination, fulfillment, or any other human value be just as valid a goal as happiness? Harris never explains, nor can he. The goal itself is outside the domain of science (could he ever falsify the goal?). We feel the desire for God, but Harris tells us it's a delusion, so why isn't our desire to promote human well-being also a delusion? Why is it a real basis for morals when he's already concluded that our desires are genetic tricks that have survival value? The idea that happiness equates to morally right is an unfounded, nonempirical matter of faith.

Second, it is simply incorrect that science can tell us what brings happiness as a matter of practice. Thousands of social issues are hotly debated precisely because equally intelligent and equally scientific people disagree about which will bring more happiness to society. Some claim that expanding the welfare state will result in greater happiness by giving resources to the poor, while others argue that it reduces happiness by making people dependent on government. Some argue that free trade brings happiness through increased prosperity, while others argue that it brings unhappiness by destroying jobs. Many social scientists have produced evidence showing that marital fidelity brings happiness, but most of the New Atheists practice sexual promiscuity on the belief that it makes them happier.[8] Both side on every issue marshal scientific arguments to make their case, yet they are as divided as ever. The hard reality is that happiness is so subjective that anything can be considered morally correct using it as a guide. There will be as many definitions of morality as there are people on the planet since everyone will have their own idea of what gives them happiness. The notion that we can just settle matters of happiness by appealing to science is somewhat naïve.

Harris might counter that the solution is to be *more* scientific. Once society further advances in knowledge, *then* there will be more

---

8   See Arthur Brooks, *Gross National Happiness* (NY: Basic, 2008).

consensus on questions of what brings happiness. Our disagreements only persist because of ignorance, but we can conquer ignorance through ever-expanding education.

Unfortunately for him, the facts say otherwise: over the past generation, society has advanced remarkably in scientific knowledge, yet at the same time has become *more* partisan, not less, and those *most* educated and informed about public issues are the most divided of all. We have become more scientific in recent years while also becoming less unified on what brings happiness.[9]

Third, plenty of immoral behaviors promote happiness. If slave defenders like John C. Calhoun were correct that African-Americans were happier under slavery than under freedom, would that justify slavery? Would a painless genocide be acceptable so long as it produced happiness for the killers? If happiness is our criterion, then slavery, genocide, and murder would all be morally correct under certain conditions, yet we all know that painless murder is still murder. Even Bertrand Russell saw that his work in philosophy "brought moments of delight, but these [were] outweighed by years of effort and depression," yet he continued to pursue truth as a moral good anyway even though it brought net unhappiness.[10]

Philosopher John Dewey, realizing this objection, tried to save his pragmatic conception of the good by saying that if people were doing immoral things, claiming that it brought them happiness, then they were mistaken—immoral acts don't *really* bring happiness.[11] But notice that Dewey was engaged in circular reasoning, not moral investigation—ethical equates to happiness only because he has redefined happiness to be synonymous with ethical. This is unscientific in the extreme: Dewey could

---

9   See, for instance, Zeke J. Miller, "How the United States is Growing More Partisan," *Time*, June 12, 2014, accessed September 29, 2016 available at time .com/2862299/how-the-united-states-is-growing-more-partisan-in-10-charts; and Thomas E. Mann and Norman J. Ornstein, *It's Even Worse Than It Looks: How the American Constitutional System Collided with the New Politics of Extremism* (NY: Basic Books, 2012).

10   Again, without any way to justify morality itself other than through direct intuition (see below for the problems with an atheist ethic of "just knowing"). Russell, *Autobiography*, 161–62.

11   See Robert Westbrook, *John Dewey and American Democracy* (Ithaca: Cornell University Press, 1991).

never find out that something previously considered wrong was actually ethically right by discovering that it promoted happiness; he would just explain it away as not true happiness and fall back on the moral rules he started out with. Happiness wasn't really his criterion of good. He was a moral absolutist posturing as a pragmatist.

Harris and Dewey's argument is essentially a variant of the old, and largely discredited, utilitarian theory of ethics, which says that the morally right thing to do is "that which does the most good for the most people."[12] But utilitarianism is especially problematic for atheists because it still runs into the moral-empirical problem. How can an empiricist appeal to the good as a basis for morality when nobody has ever seen this mysterious thing called the good?

An atheist might try to save utilitarianism by defining the good in terms of pleasure. Because there is no absolute good or evil, says the utilitarian, we should simply seek to maximize pleasure for the most people.

But pleasure is also invisible. It is a mere subjective experience like consciousness, free will, the feeling of God's reality, or the sense of self that the atheist has already dismissed as illusion. And if everything is relatively good, then that must include pleasure itself. Either moral principles are absolute (including pleasure) or they are not, in which case pleasure itself is a relative moral principle that we can ignore just like any other. In throwing out absolute morality, utilitarians destroy the pleasure principle on which their whole ethical edifice rests.

Atheists might then respond that even though we can't see pleasure, we can, using neuroimaging, see the brain activity associated with it. When the pleasure centers of the brain light up, that is objectively good, and we should therefore promote the brain activity associated with pleasurable feelings.[13]

But from a materialist framework, why is it morally preferable to have a certain part of a material object (the brain) light up and not another? What does lighting up have to do with right and wrong? Is it morally correct for a firefly to light up? How about a light bulb? How about a

---

12 According to Bentham and Mill, the founders of utilitarianism, we could determine morality by performing a "hedonic calculus" in which we would quantify the costs and benefits of each action and then, through simple arithmetic, determine which action led to the greatest net utility.

13 Harris, *The Moral Landscape.*

cigarette? If it is not morally correct for one part of a Christmas tree to glow, how can it be morally correct for one part of the cerebral cortex to glow? That brain scans can tell us which part of the brain is active is nice but morally irrelevant.[14] Pleasure, or the brain imaging associated with pleasure, cannot be a criterion of moral goodness.

Some atheists recognize these problems and reject pleasure as their utilitarian criterion of good, pointing out that goodness is deeper and richer than mere pleasure or the brain activity associated with a pleasurable feeling. But once they do this, the statement, "Morality is that which brings the greatest good to the most people" becomes a tautology since it would be using the terms *good* and *moral* interchangeably. It can be reworded to say, "Good for everyone is that which is good for everyone." This statement offers no informative content, only a play of words. Atheists making the utilitarian argument are behaving a little like the clever sociologist who went out and "proved" that all bachelors were unmarried.

Utilitarianism also fails because of human epistemic limitations. It is simply impossible for humans to know the total costs and benefits of every possible action. Only God has such omniscience, so atheist utilitarianism, ironically, requires God in order to work. This ethical theory then becomes a form of idolatry that unsuccessfully tries to convert humans into omniscient, deified calculators of value.[15]

Utilitarianism also abolishes the human rights that most of us (including atheists) hold sacred. If morality is that which does the greatest good for the greatest number, and we determine that two human lives are better than one (again, without justification under a materialist framework), then it would be correct to kill healthy humans, harvest their two kidneys, and distribute them to those who need only one to live. We should also be willing to throw out rights to freedom of belief or expression if we determine that the greater good will be achieved by silencing someone. Because we find the idea of sacrificing human rights in this way

---

14 The same could be said of pain. It is equally an invisible feeling, and the atheist has already discounted feeling as a path to knowledge.

15 There is, of course, a true, deified calculator of value—God himself. So a religious framework (in which a transcendent God defined the good and gave us the means to know it by nonempirical means) could provide the basis for utilitarian ethics. God's commandments, then, might just be the utilitarian rules that, over the long arc of history, bring the most good to the most people. Utilitarianism can work for God but not for atheists.

morally repugnant, utilitarianism is dubious from the get go. And, of course, promises and commitments become meaningless in a utilitarian framework because we can violate them any time we decided it will maximize pleasure. Cheating on a spouse, for instance, would have to be just fine for utilitarians as long as it brings more pleasure to the cheaters than sorrow to the betrayed spouses.

Some atheists try to cling to the utilitarian argument by rephrasing it in pragmatic terms, saying, "Morality is that which is most useful." But this only begs the question, "Useful for what?" Hitler's Nazi regime was certainly useful for killing Jews, Bull Connor's police brutality was useful for oppressing African-Americans, and slavery was useful for harvesting the plantation owner's cotton. Deeming something useful doesn't solve anything morally.

Other atheists change their utilitarian tune slightly and say, "Good is that which fulfills desires," but this gets us nowhere since many of our desires are evil (the desires for vanity, revenge, endless material acquisition, or murder of a rival). Humans have infinite desires, and claiming that it is moral to fulfill them would justify indulging all of our bad desires as well as our good ones.

John Dewey would often claim we can get morals from democratic practice. He never tired of saying, "Means and ends are the same." Therefore the democratic means by which we pursue goodness are themselves the goodness we should pursue.[16] Of course, Dewey never provided any empirical evidence for this strange proposition, nor could he since it is a nonempirical and logically confused statement. Too often atheists, when they fail by reasoning, try to succeed by repeating. They believe if they just say something like "mind and matter are the same" enough times, it will somehow become true.

Either atheists are consistent empiricists or they are not. If they are, then they should stop talking about invisible entities such as the good. If they are not, then they should stop hectoring religious people for believing in a nonempirical God.

---

16 See John Dewey, *Human Nature and Conduct* (NY: Henry Holt & Co., 1922), 248–55; and Robert Westbrook, *John Dewey and American Democracy* (Ithaca: Cornell University Press, 1991). John Dewey, *Theory of Valuation* (Chicago: University of Chicago Press, 1939).

MORALS FROM EVOLUTION

Many atheists, realizing the problems with utilitarianism, try to justify morals by turning to their standard explain-all theory—Darwinism. We can find morals, they say, simply by looking at the facts of evolution: those organisms that evolved for cooperation, honesty, compassion, and altruism were more likely to survive than those that did not. We call these behaviors good because such genetic dispositions help perpetuate our selfish genes.[17] "Morality evolved," says science writer Timothy Ferris, "because it promoted human survival."[18] New Atheist Matt Ridley spends a chapter of his recent book, *The Evolution of Everything*, arguing that morals evolved just like the universe, life, culture, and technology. We don't need God for morals, this view says; we only need evolutionary biology.[19]

But notice that these atheists do the opposite of what they claim. They say they are getting morals from evolution, but they are actually getting evolution from morals. That is, atheists declare certain behaviors morally correct ahead of time (compassion, fairness, cooperation) and then go back to biology to find a plausible evolutionary path for the emergence of such behaviors. They aren't *finding* morality but only telling us that what we *already consider moral* has an evolutionary history. Why are those evolved behaviors actually "good"? Atheists haven't even begun to answer this question. They have sidestepped the whole issue by assuming what they conclude. Evolutionary biology might tell us *that* our behavioral instincts have an evolutionary history, but it cannot tell us we are somehow morally obligated to follow those instincts.

All attempts to ground morals in evolution amount to ex post reasoning—beginning with an assumption and then finding evidence to justify it after the fact. The scientific method requires that conclusions follow evidence; ex post reasoning lets evidence follow conclusions. Science is about *finding out* what we don't know, but atheist moral reasoning is about justifying what we *already* know. The morals come first, the science comes second. Latter-day Saints have long understood this, but the atheist tries to convince himself that science precedes morals. The test of truth is

17   Dennett, *Breaking the Spell*, 175–88.

18   Timothy Ferris, *The Science of Liberty* (NY: HarperCollins, 2010), 280.

19   Dawkins, *The God Delusion*, 245–53.

not narrative, but prediction, and when it comes to morality, Darwinian fundamentalism spins plenty of narratives but makes no predictions. It is not, therefore, scientific.

These atheists also fail to see that the fact that something evolved tells us nothing about whether or not that something is good or bad. To Darwinian fundamentalists, evolution is a random process operating in an indifferent universe, so why are the products of that random process "moral"? Is it morally right that a monkey has a tail, simply because it evolved? Is it morally right that certain frogs are venomous, simply because they evolved that way? Is it morally right that certain humans have attached earlobes or fair skin simply because they evolved that way? We all understand that it's neither right nor good that a trait evolved. It is simply what has happened, so why do atheists say it's morally right that we evolved to cooperate or give charitably?

In this, atheists are making the classic mistake of confusing an "is" for an "ought." It doesn't follow that if something *is* a certain way, then it *ought* to be that way. This reasoning suggests that since it *is* true that we've evolved to cooperate, therefore we *ought* to cooperate. But it's also true that there *is* poverty in the United States, but it doesn't follow that there *ought* to be poverty in the United States. It *is* true that a person was murdered yesterday, but it doesn't follow that it was morally correct that this person was murdered. Saying that we *are* evolved for certain behaviors and therefore we *ought to* do those behaviors is as mistaken as saying North Korea's Kim family *is* tyrannical; therefore it is morally right that it tyrannizes. Since "is" and "ought" are radically different things, we can never find what we *should* do by looking at what it is we *actually* do—and explaining what it is we actually do is all evolutionary science is capable of.

But that's only the beginning of the problems with trying to get morals from biology. Even more devastating is this: because these Darwinian fundamentalists tell us we can know what is good by seeing what evolved, then *every behavior must be good for every behavior evolved*. If those behaviors that aided survival are moral, then it necessarily follows that every behavior is morally correct, for they all aided survival in some way. If they hadn't, the circular logic of the Darwinian fundamentalist goes, they wouldn't have persisted in the gene pool.

Since we humans have evolved to do contrary things, how can appealing to evolution help us decide which of these opposites is morally correct? For example, we've evolved the desire to get something for nothing through theft but also to respect the property of others and earn a living through honest work. We've evolved to take vengeance on those who have insulted us (even monkeys engage in honor killings) but also to forgive our enemies. We've evolved to desire the pleasure of taking drugs but also to abstain from the destruction of addictive substances. We've evolved for racism (to privilege our own genetic kinship group) but also to treat all people with respect regardless of race.

A selfish person, by grabbing more for herself, will be more likely to survive and perpetuate her selfish genes (they are selfish, after all). Why, then, is selfishness wrong if evolution is our guide to morality? A murderous tendency would aid a male in his quest to eliminate rivals and thereby gather more resources and reproductive partners for the perpetuation of his genes, yet we know that murder is wrong and forgiveness is right.

One man is programmed by evolution to be a serial rapist because it will spread his selfish genes far and wide among many women. Another man is programmed by evolution to be faithful to his wife because it ensures his offspring will be protected in a stable, loving household. If marital fidelity and serial rape are equally programmed by evolution, how can we prefer one to another if evolution is our criterion of good?[20] If honesty, compassion, and cooperation are good because they evolved, then dishonesty, cruelty, and selfishness must be equally good because they evolved too. That a behavior evolved hardly makes that behavior right or wrong, good or evil, moral or immoral. Otherwise all bad behaviors would have to be considered as morally correct as the good ones. There is no way around this for the "get morals from evolution" crowd.

The problem of trying to derive morals from evolution is on display in the writings of Richard Dawkins when he advances an argument for sexual freedom by saying, "Just as we rise above nature when we spend time writing a book or a symphony rather than devoting our time to sowing our selfish genes and fighting our rivals, so mightn't we rise above nature when tempted by the vice of sexual jealousy?"[21]

---

20 Randy Thornhill made the case that rape evolved naturally as a survival strategy in his book, *A Natural History of Rape* (Cambridge: MIT Press, 2000). Of course, from a Darwinian fundamentalist point of view, this is an incontestable fact, nonetheless, Jerry Coyne tried to argue against Thornhill's view in "The Fairy Tales of Evolutionary Psychology," *The New Republic*, March 4, 2000, 299.

21 Dawkins, "Banishing the Green-Eyed Monster," *The Washington Post Online*.

Indeed, why not? And why stop there? Why not rise above nature when tempted to be compassionate, racially sensitive, or honest? Why not rise above nature when it tells us to refrain from murder? Why not rise above nature when tempted by the "vice" of helping others? Dawkins claims sexual jealousy is a vice, but why not also compassion, charity, honesty, or any other evolved characteristic that we experience as a subjective feeling? Why does Dawkins throw out one feeling (sexual jealousy) as a vice but not others (such as charity)? Why can we throw out the evolved morals that forbid sexual promiscuity but not, say, the evolved morals that prohibit genocide? It's clear that other than his own preferences, Dawkins has no guidance for us as to when we should accede to nature or when should we rise above it. Presumably he just likes to engage in sexual promiscuity but not murder.

Every argument against *following* evolution as a basis of morality can also be made against *defying* evolution as a basis of morality. How can evolution be any kind of a guide to moral behavior when we can arbitrarily reject certain evolved morals whenever we please? Throw out moral feelings and rise above them, says Dawkins, forgetting that throwing out God doesn't just remove God's laws he doesn't like ("thou shalt not commit adultery") but those laws he does like as well ("thou shalt not kill"). Why are we bound by certain instincts but not others? The atheist has no valid answer.

Close examination reveals that atheists are not trying to justify *all* morals using evolution but only those morals they prefer (usually those aligned with intellectually fashionable politics). They have their pet moralities they cherish in the name of evolution (freedom, social justice, equality, compassion, or tolerance) and those they debunk in the name of evolution (chastity, self-restraint, patriotism, or respect). Not only is this illogical, but it is also hypocritical.[22] If we can rise above nature whenever we like, then we are back to the moral nihilism of doing whatever we want. Nietzsche, again, is proven right.[23]

---

22 I wonder if atheists have a nice evolutionary story for how hypocrisy came about—and if it has evolved, is it then good or bad?

23 This "defy evolution" approach to morality is also problematic from a materialist point of view that rejects free will as a mere illusion. According to the atheist, we can choose to defy our competitive, immoral animal nature, but what is this nonmaterial "we" that can do the nonmaterial "choosing"? Aren't the "self" and "choice" just illusions created by the brain?

Lacking any means for justifying the good other than saying that it evolved, the atheist is left to arbitrarily and retroactively cherry pick from evolution things they like and don't like. Morals become a matter of cultural prejudice, but this is hardly a legitimate ground for correct action. After all, Southern racism, medieval monarchism, and European fascism were all cultural prejudices.

Atheists often fall back on the rule to not hurt others as the essence of their moral code, but why not rise above that too? Mass murderers do. Is our distaste for Hitler and his holocaust also just another evolution-produced emotion that we can defy when we please? Members of evolving species have been hurting each other for millennia in their quest for survival. On what grounds can we now suddenly declare this wrong? Our dislike of harm is just a feeling, and atheists insist our feelings are not to be trusted. A consistent atheist would say, "Our feeling that there is a God is just a feeling. Our feeling that we have free will is just a feeling. Our feeling that racism is wrong is just a feeling. Our feeling that Hitler was evil is just a feeling." It's quite clear: a godless world is also a "goodless" world.

Richard Dawkins himself once admitted as much. While he normally waxes moralistic and chastises religious believers for all of the "evils" they bring to the world, in 1986 he wrote, "The universe we observe has precisely the properties we should expect if there is at bottom, no design, no purpose, *no evil and no good*, nothing but blind pitiless indifference" (emphasis added).[24] Remarkably, Dawkins spends much of his life trying to convince us that atheism is good and religion is evil, only to completely disavow the entire framework of good and evil in a candid moment. Why go after religion for the evils it promotes if evil doesn't even exist? That Dawkins sings one tune with scientists and another when insulting religious believers in public shows that he is fundamentally dishonest, but having already banished good and evil from the universe, why shouldn't he be? Dishonesty, after all, is just part of the illusion of morality.

What evolutionary morality gives us, then, is a mere moral tautology. Its maxim must be, "Keep doing whatever you are doing because if you are doing it, evolution must have wired you to do it; therefore, it's morally correct." This is hardly a useful guide to correct action, but it is all the atheists have. Those of us not wrapped up in the irrationalities of

---

24   Dawkins, *The Blind Watchmaker* (NY: W. W. Norton, 1986), 133.

Darwinian fundamentalism understand that "evolved" doesn't equate to "good," yet New Atheist scientists, for all of their PhDs and endowed academic chairs, refuse to face up to this obvious flaw in their moral reasoning.

MORALS FROM SURVIVAL

Some atheists try to ground morals in biology by appealing to the principle of human survival. Surely human existence is better than nonexistence, they say, so anything that perpetuates the survival of our species is right, while anything destructive to our species is wrong. We are thus morally obligated to do what enhances human survival. In this way, we simply carry Darwinism into the present: survival has been good in the past, so survival is good now. We should "help Darwinism along," as it were.

But if evolution is a random and meaningless process that just happens to operate in our universe, why is it moral to aid this random process in producing a random outcome? If the wind is blowing sand east to west, is it then morally right to pick up grains of sand and move them westward? If Mount Everest is getting slightly taller each year through plate tectonics, is it morally right to help that process along by dumping rocks on top of the world's highest peak? If not, then why is it morally correct to aid biology in carrying out its random processes of mutation and selection? Helping nature do what nature has been doing is an empty criterion of morality. There is no good or bad about survival; it is just what happens to have occurred randomly.

And if evolution is a scientific law (and we are puppets of genetics and environment), then we can't *help* but obey it, just as we can't help but obey the law of gravity. An apple falling from a tree is neither moral nor immoral; it is just an object acted upon by nature. Likewise, in a materialist framework, a human following her instincts is neither moral nor immoral; she is just an object acted upon by nature. To say that it's morally right to follow evolution (by promoting survival) is as problematic as saying that it's morally right to follow the law of gravity (meaning, presumably, that it's immoral to fly in an airplane). Just because a scientific law is in place, following that scientific law—as if we could do otherwise in a materialist framework—cannot be good or evil; it just *is*.

Survival as a basis for morality also runs up against a crucial epistemic fact: we don't know the future. According to Darwinian fundamentalism, we can only know what promotes survival *after the fact*—evolution is a process that has no foresight or plan. It operates randomly on matter, and we can only see what it selected and what was valuable for survival by looking to the past. Mutations, the biologists tell us, are wonderful, unanticipated surprises that jump out of nowhere to give advantages to species. For example, the mutation that gave colorful feathers to the peacock ostensibly helps their selfish genes survive by attracting mates, but we would have thought that it would have reduced peacock survival by making them more visible to predators. The benefit of a given mutation is only known retroactively. Despite all of the progressive rhetoric to the contrary, we can't tell the future, and we can't know which mutations will promote survival until after they have been tried. It is impossible to "help evolution along" because we have no idea where it is going.[25]

In the early twentieth century, Marxist political ideology seemed future-oriented and progressive to many atheists, but we know in retrospect that it was an unmitigated disaster for humanity. Millions of capable people who could have aided human survival by making discoveries in medicine, science, or technology starved in Mao's famines, died in Stalin's gulags, or wound up in Pol Pot's killing fields. We only know this from the perspective of the twenty-first century but had no way to anticipate it in the nineteenth.

Which of all courses of action will promote survival? The only honest answer is, we'll see. It may turn out in a million years that those genetically predisposed to generosity were more likely to survive, but it may just as well turn out that those genetically predisposed to stinginess were more likely to survive. Only those living millions of years from now will know. It is unscientific hubris to claim that we can know where evolution is going, and it is nonsensical to claim that it's ethically right to help it along. By its own logic, Darwinism makes an ethic of promoting survival impossible.

But for the sake of argument, let's pretend for a moment that we could tell which actions were more likely to aid the survival of the species. Would that get us closer to morality? Hardly. Thousands of activities

---

25 Dawkins's "blind watchmaker" analogy only underscores the point. It would make no sense to help a blind man wandering without a purpose to reach his destination.

are morally reprehensible and would have a good chance of enhancing human survival. For example, what better way to help the species survive than removing the most unfit from the population and redirecting the resources they would have consumed to those who are more likely to produce healthy, intelligent, sturdy offspring? Every society uses massive amounts of its GDP to keep the elderly alive, even though they are well beyond childbearing years and add nothing to the survival probability of the human race. If we were really to use the "ethic of survival of the species" as our guide we ought to have them all eliminated.[26] How can we justify care for the elderly with human survival as our ethical guide?

And why stop there? The human race as a whole would be more likely to survive if we also exterminated the sterile, mentally handicapped, and terminally ill. On what grounds could we forbid such a survival-enhancing genocide? Better to save the precious resources and space of our planet for those with the fittest genes by eliminating the "less fit."[27]

Or how could we condemn any successful genocide for that matter? If what survives is morally right, then those races that lived on and eliminated their rivals through systematic slaughter would have to be deemed morally correct. That's the only reason you and I are here—our distant ancestors killed off rival tribes, thus living on while their enemies perished. The only criterion for whether genocide is moral, then, must be whether it succeeded. Yet how many atheists are willing to accept this conclusion?

The survival ethic would also make it morally appropriate for a middle-aged man to leave his wife of the same age (who is past childbearing years) and run off with a younger woman who could still perpetuate his genes. That would be a far more survival-friendly strategy than marital fidelity, yet most of us condemn such behavior as selfish and immoral. If survival is our guide, there's no reason this would be so.

---

26 The atheist might say, "Well, I wouldn't want people to eliminate *me* from the gene pool if I become unfit," but since when have morals become a matter of what you want? We can't one moment say that survival is the criterion of morality and then in the next switch it to "what I want." Wants, from the Darwinian point of view, are irrelevant to morals.

27 This mentality has already begun to bear tragic fruit. The deaths of countless Down syndrome children aborted in the womb have been justified using this logic.

The ethic of survival could also mandate that we persecute, repress, and even do away with those with homosexual inclinations. Closeted homosexuals who marry women and have children will perpetuate their selfish genes; practicing homosexuals will not. If we should do what best advances the survival of the species, then wouldn't it be right to discourage homosexuality through ridicule, persecution, and shame? On what grounds, then, do atheists applaud the gay rights movement, which advocates the opposite?[28]

Nor can a Darwinian fundamentalist logically oppose the death penalty. Executing all criminals would provide an easy way to remove defective DNA from the gene pool. Why do atheists continue to advocate the Christian morality of mercy and "turn the other cheek" when it so brazenly defies Darwinian logic?

Once we claim that Darwinism rules human life just as it rules that of all other animals, then anything not furthering survival of the fittest is, by definition, furthering the survival of the unfittest. This, in Darwinian terms, is an unnatural preservation of the less desirable people, institutions, and genes simply for the sake of preserving them—something contrary to the natural order atheists tell us to submit to.

Atheists commonly condemn social Darwinism—applying survival of the fittest to the human realm—as a perversion of Darwin's actual theory. But why? If, as they claim, Darwinism is a law that governs biology and humans are mere biological creatures, how can applying Darwinism to humans be wrong? Is the application of Newton's theory to humans a perversion of physics? If nature's only rule is survival of the fittest and humans are a mere extension of nature, then we simply can't exempt ourselves from nature's Darwinian rules. That would be unmaterialist. In the name of consistency, atheists must stop running from social Darwinism and accept that it is the necessary outcome of their Darwinian fundamentalist logic.

Atheists sometimes say that Hitler abused Darwinism in practicing his anti-Semitic eugenics. Perhaps he did, but so does anyone who derives ethics from biology. Hitler drew a false morality from Darwinism, but so do all materialist scientists today who pick the ethics they like, invent a plausible story about how they might have emerged through natural selection, and then dub them ethical simply because they now have a story (no matter how dubious) of how it might have come about.

---

28   Dawkins, *The God Delusion*, 326–27.

Not only does survival fail as a criterion of morality, but were we to adopt it (irony of ironies), atheism itself would have to be considered immoral. The Darwinian fundamentalists tell us that evolution has wired us to believe in God, so if we are morally bound to do what evolution has wired us to do, then believe in God we must. The genes of religious people are also much more likely to survive than those of atheists simply because the religious have far more children. If we must follow the survival criterion of morality, then everyone is morally obligated to become a Mormon and produce a Mormon-sized family. Atheism is a clear loser when it comes to the long-term survival of the species. So if morality hinges on survival, we should all flee atheism immediately as a moral imperative.

And if we should do what brings the most happiness, we should be religious, since plenty of research has shown that religious people are happier than nonreligious people.[29] If, as Sam Harris contends, science can objectively show us what brings happiness and we *should* do whatever it finds, then isn't it objectively true that we *should* be religious and therefore reject everything Harris says? And isn't Harris himself behaving immorally by attacking religion since such actions objectively diminish happiness? The contradictions that pile up when one adopts a materialist philosophy are staggering.

The reality is that morality doesn't come by acceding to evolution but usually by defying it. Atheists often tell a happy story (usually culminating in the Scopes Trial of 1925) of how Darwinism killed God. Novelist Tom Wolfe has pointed out that actually, God killed Darwinism.[30] That is, at some point in history, humans developed religion, and their God (or gods) told them *not* to apply the ruthless law of survival of the fittest that governs all other parts of the animal kingdom. A belief in God turned men away from mere survival and toward the very un-Darwinian principles of compassion, forgiveness, self-sacrifice, love, and tolerance. Atheists attempt to ground morals in survival, but it is precisely the rejection of survival that sets humans morally apart from other animals.

Even Thomas Huxley, the greatest nineteenth-century advocate of Darwin's theory, recognized that we don't get morality *from* evolution but that our morality pits us *against* evolution. He said:

29   For more on the link between religion and happiness, see chapter 8.

30   Tom Wolfe, "The Human Beast," 2006 NEH Jefferson lecture, May 9, 2006.

The practice of that which is ethically best—what we call goodness or virtue—involves a course of conduct which, in all respects, is opposed to that which leads to success in the cosmic struggle for existence. In place of ruthless self-assertion it demands self-restraint; in place of thrusting aside, or treading down, all competitors, it requires that the individual shall not merely respect, but shall help his fellows; its influence is directed, not so much to the survival of the fittest, as to the fitting of as many as possible to survive.[31]

We don't get morality from Darwinism because morals usually tell us to do the opposite of what Darwinism dictates. Darwin himself recognized this, but too many of his modern-day disciples do not.[32]

We find the same atheist contradiction when it comes to meaning in life. The religious sometimes point out that if the materialist worldview were correct, then life and the universe would have no meaning. Some atheists angrily retort that it doesn't matter if the universe has no meaning so long as *people* do, and that's good enough.

But once again, look at the sleight of hand they pull. With other evolved sensibilities, such as belief in God or certain traditional morals, the atheist insists that our evolved beliefs are illusions and we can ignore them as we wish ("rise above nature" in Dawkins's words[33]). But then they solemnly proclaim that our evolved belief in meaning is sacred, real, and must be cherished. Why should we cling to one evolutionary illusion (meaning) but ridicule another (God, free will, or certain morals)? This is something atheists are unable to explain. When it suits them, many atheists claim that we are mere animals, but when it comes to morals and meaning, they claim human beings are special and have the ability to direct evolution like gods. They throw the true God out the front door and sneak a new human god in through the back door. It's a kind of idolatry—a worship of one's own cultural prejudices.

---

31 Thomas Huxley, "Evolution and Ethics," The Romanes lecture, 1893, in Collected Essays of Thomas Huxley, vol. 9, accessed May 15, 2016, available at aleph0.clarku.edu/huxley/CE9/E-E.html.

32 For more on the problems of using "defy evolution" as a guide to behavior, see Appendix.

33 Dawkins, "Banishing the Green-Eyed Monster," *The Washington Post Online*.

MORALS FROM SENTIMENT

Another attempt to save evolutionary morality is to invoke evolved sentiment. Atheists will point out that we feel good helping others, and this should lead us to compassion, cooperation, kindness, and other moral traits. According to atheist Matt Ridley, "Nothing gives us [humans] more pleasure than to see others benefit."[34]

But notice that Ridley is here equating "moral" with that which gives us pleasure. In other words, for Ridley something is right if it makes us feel good. This would mean that torture is moral for a sadist, theft moral for the kleptomaniac, and murder moral for the sociopath. While it might make Ridley feel good to help others, it makes countless other humans feel good to harm others. If feeling good is our criterion of morality, we are in trouble because most people commit immoral acts on the belief that it will give them pleasure.[35]

It's plain that many, if not most, human beings derive great pleasure from doing things that cause harm to others. Ridley, the rational optimist, is unwilling to face up to the obvious. "I like" does not mean "thou shalt," and enjoying the indulgence of certain evolved instincts doesn't give those instincts moral standing. Ethics from sentiment fails quite spectacularly and was refuted by philosopher David Hume almost three centuries ago, yet New Atheists continue to trot it out as if it is somehow original.

MORALS FROM INTUITION

Related to ethics from sentiment is ethics from intuition. Atheists often say that we "just know" when something is right or wrong. It's a gut instinct thing. This is where Sam Harris retreats to when pressed: people just intuitively know that the "good life," as he describes it, is better than

---

34 Ridley, "The Evolution of Morality," in *The Evolution of Everything*. He paraphrases Adam Smith in claiming we get morals from "evolved sentiment."

35 We can no more get morality from Darwin's theory of biology than we can get it from Adam Smith's theory of economics. The Wealth of Nations told us how exchange happens, but it would be foolish to say that "whatever exchange produces is morally right" since that, of course, would make the purchase of slaves, drugs, sexual acts, etc. into "moral" activities. Exchange no more makes something right than does survival.

the "bad life."[36] Likewise, John Dewey ultimately confessed that good and evil were just a given. He didn't need science or any philosophy to "enable him to distinguish between, say, the good of kindness and the evil of slander." The superiority of love to hate, democracy to dictatorship, and other basic moral principles were "simply experienced." They were the starting point of his philosophy, not the conclusion.[37] We don't need God for morality, atheists say, we just need our moral intuitions.

By invoking intuition, atheists are once again caught in self-contradiction. By invoking "just knowing," the atheist has thrown out the empiricism on which his atheism rests. When religious people claim they just know something without sensory evidence, the atheist starts talking about flying spaghetti monsters. When atheists claim to just know what is morally right without sensory evidence, they think it's acceptable. Both the just knowing there is a God and just knowing what is right, according to the materialist framework, must be mere chemical states of the brain, not sources of truth. If the atheist has invalidated any kind of extrasensory knowledge as illegitimate, then he can't suddenly bring it back when it is convenient.

Bertrand Russell advanced a version of the morals from the "just knowing" argument, saying moral intuitions are given in the concrete facts of everyday experience. He said, "We see goodness and badness in things as we see their colors and shapes."[38] But how is this different from the religious claim that we see God in everyday experience? Some look across the expanse of the Grand Canyon and claim they see God there as plainly evident as the canyon's color and shape. Russell's experience of "the good" isn't objective; it's a subjective experience unique to him, just like the feelings of God that religious believers have when they look up to the starry heavens. If we can just experience the good through the intuitions of common experience, why can't we also just experience God in the same way? Russell, the atheist, has no consistent answer.

How many ex-Mormon atheists, when reminded of times they felt God or the Spirit, now say, "Yes, but those were just feelings"? Yet when

---

36   Harris, *Moral Landscape*, 15–17.

37   See Westbrook, *John Dewey*, 143.

38   Russell, *Autobiography*, 161.

it comes to morality, they accept "just feelings" as a guide to right action and a legitimate path to knowledge. Do they see the contradiction? Either we can know things through nonempirical means—in which case both God and good can be known by intuition (revelation)—or we cannot—in which case the Good Delusion is as real as the God Delusion. No God means no good.

MORAL RELATIVISM?

Given all of the above problems with empiricist-materialist morality, the atheist must finally retreat into the refuge of relativism. This view says that, in fact, there are no absolute morals. What is right and wrong depends entirely upon the situation. What is considered right in one time and place may not be considered right in another. For instance, Matt Ridley points out that two hundred years ago it was acceptable to hold slaves in America, but today it is not. Our morality has evolved along with science.

This concept is puzzling. Does Ridley really believe that Southern slaveholders were as morally correct as the Northern abolitionists? Does Ridley really think that neither side was right in the Civil War and that the proslavery forces, in their evolved morality, were just as correct as the antislavery forces in their evolved morality? Does he really think that if the proslavery side had won and we had evolved to accept slavery, then slavery would today be morally correct? I doubt it.

Ridley and other atheists fall into the error of relativism because they confuse *knowledge* of something with the *nature* of that something. Ten thousand years ago people thought the earth was flat, but we now know it is round. The *nature* of the earth didn't change. Only our *knowledge* of it did. Likewise, our *knowledge* of morals might change, but the *nature* of morality does not. Moral truths are absolute (timeless and unchanging) even if our knowledge of them is not. That certain people didn't *know* slavery was immoral is irrelevant—the *nature* of slavery was, is, and always will be morally wrong.

Many also claim to be relativists because they misunderstand what relativism is. They say that since it would be correct to lie to Nazi soldiers in order to protect Jews hiding in your home, lying is wrong under some circumstances but not others. Therefore, morality is relative.

But this isn't relativism. It's simply choosing the lesser of two (absolute) evils. It is absolutely wrong to lie and also absolutely wrong to cooperate with genocide, but you must do one or the other. You must commit an evil to prevent a greater evil. It's not that lying is good, only that cooperating in genocide is worse. I've met hundreds of people in my life who professed to be moral relativists, but I've never met an actual moral relativist. When pressed, everyone admits that at least their own preferred morals are absolute.[39]

CONCLUSION

In a conversation with a young atheist awhile back, I asked, "If there is no God, then where do you get your morals from?"

He replied, "That's easy: moral is whatever does the most good for the most people."

I answered, "But if you can just make up this morality (or learn it from someone else who made it up), then why can't I make up my own morality as well? If you can just invent a morality of 'do the most good for the most people,' why can't I just invent a morality of, 'do the most good for myself' or 'dominate others' or 'seek the greatness of my racial group'?"

At this point he didn't have an answer. He might have tried to say he didn't invent these morals—that they came from a higher source, but this would then lead to the question, what is that higher source? If we just invent our own morality, then we have no reason for obeying it. If morality comes from a higher source, then this leads us straight to *the* Source of all truth, goodness, and beauty—God Himself.

The above should make clear this crucial point: atheism offers no guidance when it comes to morality. That fixed moral precepts can never be found in contingent science is something religious people have been

---

39   Some Latter-day Saints interpret 1 Nephi 4 as a justification of moral relativism, pointing out that, under the circumstances, it was right for Nephi to "murder" Laban. I disagree. Murder is the taking of innocent life, but Laban had stolen Nephi's family property and was engaged in a campaign to kill him and his brothers. Under most theories of just violence, killing to protect innocent life (including one's own) is justified as self-defense. Rather than committing murder, Nephi protected himself and his family *from* a murderer. Perhaps 1 Nephi 4 provides as much an argument for self-defense as it does for utilitarian ethics.

saying all along but what the atheist refuses to admit.[40] Atheists don't get morals from evolution but start with morals and then justify them after the fact by inventing evolutionary stories. This is not science but faith.

Since good and evil are beyond the domain of materialist-empiricism, morality is not a gap in what science *has* explained. It's a limit on what science *can* explain. From the materialist-empiricist point of view, morals are as unscientific and unwarranted as belief in God. Scientists such as Stephen J. Gould and Henry Eyring have come to accept this limitation on science, but the New Atheists largely refuse to face up to the implications of their philosophy.[41] Dostoyevsky famously declared, "Without God, everything is permitted." It appears he was correct. Atheists must accept the fact that if there is a God delusion, because evolution has tricked us into believing in divinity, then there is equally a "good delusion" because evolution has tricked us into believing in morality. Atheists wanting a godless world must prepare themselves to live in a goodless world as well.

---

40 Science writer Timothy Ferris, an advocate of the materialist worldview, even concedes that the human rights on which his liberal politics are based are not subject to change. But if they are fixed, how can they be established as scientific conclusions which are, by definition, never fixed?

41 See Stephen Jay Gould, "Nonoverlapping Magisteria," *Natural History* 106 (March 1997): 16–22; and Henry Eyring, *The Faith of a Scientist* (Salt Lake City: Bookcraft, 1967). A few more brave atheists are "coming out" and facing up to this fact. Yuval Noah Harari, in his book *Sapiens* (NY: Harper, 2015), claims that there is no such thing as God, right, wrong, commandments, or human rights. They are all fictions created by humans to preserve social order. While I recoil at the bleak view Harari presents, I applaud his honesty in speaking clearly about the implications of materialism.

Chapter 8

THE VALUE OF GOD

WHILE THE PREVIOUS CHAPTER SHOWED that philosophically, materialist-empiricism has no means by which to justify morality, this chapter will show that the connection between God and the good is more than theoretical. There is strong, abundant empirical evidence to back it up. Religion produces morality and happiness in both individuals and society. It would be a mistake, from a practical point of view alone, for societies to adopt the atheist position.

Atheists have always denied that religion is *truthful*, but the New Atheists of the twenty-first century are extra vocal in denying that it is *useful*.[1] September 11, 2001, seems to have been a turning point. With radical Muslims responsible for the murder of more than three thousand innocent Americans, atheists turned militant in their antireligion views.[2] Today, they frequently quote physicist Steven Weinberg who said, "Religion is an insult to human dignity. With or without it you would have good people doing good things and evil people doing evil things. But for good people to do evil things, that takes religion."[3]

For many atheists, religious belief is *the* central force for evil in the world.

---

1   Dennett, *Breaking the Spell*, 44–45.

2   What about Muslim violence? This is a trickier and more complicated question than previously thought. One recent study suggests that there is less violence, murder, and suicide in Muslim countries than in less religious ones. See Don Soo Chon, "National Religious Affiliation and Integrated Model of Homicide and Suicide," *Homicide Studies* vol. 21, no. 1, February 29, 2016, 39–58.

3   Quoted at Freedom from Religion website, accessed August 18, 2016. ffrf.org /outreach/awards/emperor-has-no-clothes-award/item/11907-steven-weinberg.

To prove the point, the New Atheists have begun digging into the past and rehashing all of the wickedness done in God's name throughout the centuries. This includes, of course, the medieval inquisitions, the persecution of Galileo and other scientists, the Salem witch hunt, Christian Crusades, religious wars, and now Islamic terrorism.[4] They even delve into Mormon history, bringing up the Mountain Meadows Massacre, the Dan Lafferty murders, and Danite conspiracies.[5]

THEY HAVE IT BACKWARD

Yet in all of their antireligious diatribes, the "scientific" atheists fail to ask a basic and crucial scientific question: is religion the *cause* of all this violence? Is faith really the problem, or are *people* the problem? Isn't it more likely that humans are naturally violent and that religious teachings of love, mercy, and forgiveness actually help tame those natural impulses?

To answer this question, we must move beyond the atheist point that religious people have done most of the violence in history simply because believers have always vastly outnumbered atheists, so it could hardly be otherwise. To test whether religion was the cause of violence, we would have to control for the religious variable by comparing the per capita violence committed by religious believers to the per capita violence committed by atheists.

It just so happens that history has provided us with natural experiments whereby we can make such a comparison. We can look at those few situations in history where atheists have gotten exactly what they wanted—overtly atheistic regimes purged of religion—and then contrast them to the religious regimes of the time.

When we do this, we find that the atheists have it exactly backward: *atheism is far more likely to produce violence than religion.* And it's not even close. When humanity has created atheistic societies, they have been unmitigated disasters.

---

4   See especially Harris, *The End of Faith*, 80–152; Hitchens, God Is Not Great, chapters 1 and 2, and pages 173–93.

5   See, for instance, Jon Krakauer, *Under the Banner of Heaven: A Story of Violent Faith* (NY: Random House, 2003). Much has been made of the inquisition of Galileo, but recent historical research has shown that the "science versus religion" interpretation of the event is terribly misleading. The fate of Galileo had as much to do with personal vendettas and politics as it did religion. See Numbers, ed., *Galileo Goes to Jail.*

Communism, a "scientific" philosophy premised on atheistic materialism,[6] resulted in the deaths of more than one hundred million people in the twentieth century alone. Stalin's massacre of tens of millions of his own people in summary executions or Gulag slave labor is well-known.[7] Cambodian Communist dictator Pol Pot carried out one of the worst per capita state-sponsored slaughters in history, killing up to a quarter of the Cambodian people under the banner of his atheist philosophy. In numerical terms, Mao's Communist China was the worst of all. He had millions directly killed, and some forty-five million more starved to death in his man-made famine. His Cultural Revolution was the most extensive and violent witch hunt in world history.

With such a death toll on the atheist side of the ledger, it really is time to put to bed the idea that societies would be better off without religion. Atheists, acting in the name of science, have done far more per-capita violence than believers acting in the name of God. Historical fact has decidedly disproven the notion that a world without God is a world without violence.[8]

That atheists often deny this shows how unscientific certain scientific materialists can be. Anecdotal evidence is not scientific evidence, yet anecdotes (a handful of stories) are all the atheists have in their condemnations of religion. The claims of Hitchens, Dawkins, Harris, Dennett, and Weinberg are exercises in wishful thinking. The verdict is in, and it's clear: despite the violence done in the name of religion, the violence done in the name of atheism is far worse.

NOT REALLY ATHEISTS?

At this point, New Atheists respond that this killing in the name of atheistic science wasn't true atheism or science but a perversion of both.

6   Marx openly called his philosophy materialism (specifically dialectical materialism), and his rejection of God was the starting point of his whole philosophy.

7   See Anne Applebaum, *Gulag: A History* (NY: Penguin, 2004).

8   For a small sample of the literature on atheist violence, see Jean-Louis Panné, et. al., *The Black Book of Communism* (Cambridge: Harvard University Press, 1997); Paul Johnson, *Modern Times* (NY: HarperCollins, 1991); Jung Chang, *Mao: The Unknown Story* (London: Jonathan Cape, 2005), and *Wild Swans* (NY: Doubleday, 1991).

Communism, they say, wasn't really scientific, even though Marx and his disciples claimed it was.[9]

If we can excuse horrors committed in the name of science as not "true science," can't we just as easily excuse all of the horrors committed in the name of religion as not "true religion"? Just as most atheists would disavow all scientific violence as perversions of true science, so most religious people I know would disavow all religious violence as perversions of true religion. If we can classify someone as "not one of us" when we don't like what they do, then it must apply to religion as well as atheism.

In another attempt to dismiss the violent track record of anti-God regimes, atheists will engage in some verbal maneuvering, claiming that atheistic dictators actually *were* religious (despite their open disavowals of religion). Communists, say some atheists, claimed to reject God, but their dogmatic commitment to ideology made them believers in a new political god. A true atheism, they say, would dispense with all dogmas, including ideological ones. Stalin, Mao, and Pol Pot were not true atheists but secret religious impostors claiming to be atheists.[10]

But if atheists can simply declare someone not a true atheist whenever they don't like what they do, why can't Christians or Muslims declare someone not a true religious believer on the same grounds? Can't we say that the inquisitors, with their intolerance, bigotry, and lack of humanity, were not *truly* Christians? Can't we declare witch hunters in Salem to have been guided by an uncharitable, pharisaical zeal that went contrary to the teachings of Christ? Can't we declare all violent Islamic extremists as not true Muslims because they are violating the tenets of peace that are at the core of the Muslim faith? If atheists are only true atheists when they do things atheists like, then we can just as easily claim that religious believers are only true religious believers when they do things that religious believers like. Consistency demands that if we must accept that crimes committed in the name of religion were motivated by religion, then we must also accept that crimes committed in the name of atheism were motivated by atheism.

On the other hand, if we want to say that Communists, Nazis, and other ideologues were religious because faith is hardwired into the human psyche and everyone, even atheists, are religious in a fundamental sense,

9   See, for instance, Dawkins, *The God Delusion*, 308–15.

10   Ibid.

then I would agree. All people have faith commitments to unseen ideals. Man, in the words of sociologist Will Herberg, is *homo religious*—a religious being by nature who needs some higher purpose to give his life meaning. Humans must worship something, said T. S. Eliot, and if we don't worship God then we will bow down before idols of gold, or wood, or ideas.[11] There is no way out of faith and worship; there is only a choice of *what* we worship.[12]

The Old Testament didn't warn of godlessness, but it did warn of idolatry because that's the only real alternative. We all need something for which to live and something for which to die. If we don't find it in belief in the true God, we will find it in material acquisition, careers, or political ideologies. No wonder partisan bickering in America has increased as religion has decreased over the past generation: for many, political parties have become "Churches built up, but not unto the Lord" (2 Nephi 28:3), and ideologies have become creeds. As the myth of the saved versus the damned wanes, the myth of the left versus the right fills the void. Americans have created secular gods to replace the God of the Bible.

So the question is not, "Should we have a religion?" Rather it is, "What kind of religion should we have?" Since atheistic faiths are far more violent than those that recognize God, we are left to conclude that God-based religion is not a net cause of violence but a restraint on the natural violent impulses built into human nature.[13] The Founding Fathers and Alexis de Tocqueville wisely foresaw the consequences of atheistic regimes of the twentieth century and urged Americans to hold fast to morality and religion as the natural supports of free societies.[14]

---

11   See Will Herberg, *Judaism and Modern Man* (NY: Atheneum, 1977).

12   For more on this and the faith of atheists, see chapter four.

13   Even the secular humanist scholar and journalist Fareed Zakaria saw the important role churches have historically played in restraining tyranny. Zakaria, *The Future of Freedom* (NY: Norton, 2003).

14   See, for instance, Tocqueville's *Democracy in America* (1835) and George Washington's 1789 Farewell Address.

INDIVIDUAL GOODNESS

Belief in God restrains evil on both a societal and a personal level. While the New Atheists claim (without evidence) that religious superstition turns people into stingy, dishonest, violent, unhappy bigots, we all know, through individual experience, that this is untrue. The religious people we associate with are, by and large, motivated by their faith to give benevolently, volunteer time, give service, and live decent, moral lives. We Latter-day Saints see this first hand in our local congregations and stakes. Most of us can also personally attest to being at our most charitable when we are at our most believing. The atheist wants us to indulge our generous instincts and deny our religious ones, but the two go together. Given what we learned about the "good delusion," this shouldn't be surprising.

But we don't have to rely on personal experience or theology alone to know the value of religion; social science bears it out too. Study after study confirms our intuition that religious people are more honest, law-abiding, generous, selfless, and charitable (in both time and money) than are the less religious.[15] Highly religious communities even have higher social capital than more secular ones.[16] All of this is particularly true of LDS communities, something that scholarship is revealing more and more.[17]

---

15   Controlling for other variables, churchgoers are far less violent and prone to crime than the nonreligious. Beauregard and O'Leary, *The Spiritual Brain*, 247; and the entire October/November 2003 issue of *American Enterprise* magazine entitled, "Things Go Better with God," accessed July 5, 2016, available at www .unz.org/Pub/AmEnterprise/?Period=2003_10. See Arthur Brooks, "Religious Faith and Charitable Giving," *Policy Review*, October 1, 2003, accessed December 16, 2015. www.hoover.org/research/religious-faith-and-charitable -giving. See Beauregard and O'Leary, *The Spiritual Brain*, 247.

16   For the contribution of religion to social capital, see Robert Putnam and David Campbell, *American Grace* (NY: Simon & Schuster, 2010); and Laurence R. Iannaccone, "Religious Participation: A Human Capital Approach," *Journal for the Scientific Study of Religion* vol. 29, no. 3, (September 1990): 297–314.

17   See, for instance, James T. Duke, ed., *Latter-Day Saint Social Life, Social Research on the LDS Church and its Members* (Provo, Utah: BYU Religious Studies Center, 1998); and Lee Davidson, "Utah Has Nation's Lowest Income Inequality," *Salt Lake Tribune*, October 27, 2011, accessed November 23, 2016, available at archive.sltrib.com/story.php?ref=/sltrib/politics/52790774-90/utah-income-inequality-among.html.csp.

GOD AND THE GOOD

Why do believers (particularly Mormons) generally demonstrate higher morality, on both an individual and societal level, than secularists? The restored gospel gives five particularly strong answers that I've summarized below.

1. Dignity

While materialism cannot make a fundamental distinction between man and matter, the gospel can. The LDS view places humans above all else in nature in a unique category of value. God has created us in His image and bestowed upon us a special dignity. Humans are more than matter; they are children of God with infinite worth.

This is a central lesson taught in the book of Genesis. Human bodies were created of the "dust of the earth" (matter), but into this material vessel God placed a spirit. This spiritual nature makes us coeternal with God and means that we have the potential for eternal life, or life like God's (see D&C 19:4–12).[18] In the gospel view, we are godly *subjects*, not mere material *objects*.

Since most evil comes down to treating human beings like objects, this has crucial implications for morality. Slavery treats humans as possessions to be owned, murder treats humans as animals to be slaughtered, pornography treats humans as figures to be lusted after, theft treats humans as sources of money to be exploited, and so forth. Materialism can only reinforce the objectification of people because it, by definition, conceives of people as nothing more than material objects.

Sam Harris is adamant that his conception of morality requires that we seek the well-being of conscious creatures. But why? From a materialist point of view, consciousness is an evolution-produced illusion. Why does he get to arbitrarily decide that the illusion of consciousness bestows some special status on material objects?

With the dignity bestowed by God, however, humans can demand that we be respected as something higher than an object. Those who treat us as things to be acted upon instead of things to act (see 2 Nephi 2:14) violate and insult our basic nature.

---

18   Joseph Smith, "The King Follett Discourse."

2. Accountability

The gospel also sustains morality because it teaches that God holds us *accountable* for our actions. Death is not the end. We will live beyond mortality to be judged by God for our deeds. There is reward, punishment, and just recompense for what we've done.

If, on the other hand, the atheists are right and there is no God or afterlife, then as long as we are not caught, we will never be held accountable for our evil actions. Stalin and Mao, for instance, were never punished for their genocides, so, under atheism, they simply got away with them. All of us obey human laws for fear of punishment, but only believers in God accept that there is a divine punishment that keeps us obeying moral laws even when there is no earthly prohibition or punishment.

In the absence of God as a divine judge, atheists are left appealing to history for accountability. However, history is a poor judge because everyone escapes its sentence with death. In the materialist view, once we are gone and annihilated, we won't be around to care what history says. If we die before punishment for our evil deeds, we will feel no shame or dishonor from history because we will not survive beyond our lifetimes to see history unfold. But if there is a God and an immortal soul, we will eventually face God (and history's) verdict. Marx tried to turn history into a god (conceiving of history as a force of supreme power that moved humanity toward utopia), but it didn't work for him and it doesn't work for atheists now.

3. Ontology

The gospel also gives transcendent ontological status to morals. That is, morals have an existence and reality independent of humans—they are not artificial. We don't invent moral truths, and we can't alter or abolish them. "Truth is independent" of our perceptions of that truth, according to Doctrine and Covenants 93, so moral laws are as real and fixed as any physical law. They are not relative to time and place and are not subject to change (although the applications of moral laws may be). God is the giver of laws, and His existence and goodness make ethical norms real and binding. They have an independent, eternal status.

Under atheism, on the other hand, human beings invent moral precepts. They are something either biology or humans create (is there a distinction in the atheist view?). Moral laws are positive and artificial rather than natural and therefore as arbitrary and fleeting as the laws of fashion, which change with the whims of opinion or the laws of nations that change with new legislation.

If moral rules are just artificial conventions invented for human use, they can be ignored or altered at our convenience. They can have no more demands on us than any other made-up rules—such as the rules of dinner etiquette. If we can change the rules of manners to suit our preferences, why not also change the rules of morality that we equally invented? If morals evolve, then what's wrong with letting them evolve in, say, a fascist direction? If our sense of right and wrong can change to sanction the killing of unborn children, why can't they also evolve to permit the wholesale slaughter of a racial group? Atheists have already tethered themselves to the idea that morals evolve, so they cannot reject any new evolutions that may yet come about.

Of course, the atheist likely won't admit that he is just following fashions but will create a scientific theory of morals to fit the new evolutions. He falls in line with the morals *du jour* and then cooks up an ethical theory to match. In this, atheists are mistaking storytelling for science—an example of the narrative fallacy. Under normal circumstances, scientists understand this is impermissible, but when it comes to morality, they are all too willing to violate their own scientific standards.

And that the morals yielded by atheist scientific ethics just happen to match culturally progressive fads on every point (abortion, gay marriage, military action, and so on) underscores just how beholden to fashion atheist morals are.[19] Science is about surprise and discovery—going from the unknown to the known—but the "scientific" morality of atheists simply justifies what they already want to believe and do.

What will atheists say when bigotry becomes fashionable? We already have an idea, because religious bigotry has risen in certain sectors of society. The Broadway musical, *The Book of Mormon*, singles out and ridicules an entire faith group, yet the New Atheists have no problem supporting and patronizing this play since it is currently fashionable to do so. Trendy morals have evolved toward religious prejudice, and we can expect more of the same so long as fads, rather than independent truth, are the basis for what society considers right.

---

19 The almost uniformly progressive political views of the New Atheists are visible throughout their books and op-eds, although Hitchens and Harris do break from the left on antiterrorism policy.

Can atheists act morally? Certainly, just as you and I can follow the conventions of table manners, but if table manners change, you and I will change our behavior along with them, and once moral fashions change, atheists will predictably change their ethics as well. Christopher Hitchens often challenged Christians to "name one moral act you can do that I cannot." But, of course, nobody says he could not do moral acts that others could, only that he had no ultimate reason to. His morals were just a matter of convention and if the conventions of morality changed, then the atheist, not believing in transcendent, ontologically independent morality, would go ahead and change with them.

Unlike atheists, Mormons are commanded to do what is right regardless of its popularity. Church members have already had to endure calumny, vilification, and even job loss for sticking to moral principles with regard to the nature of marriage and the sanctity of life. Mormons understand that we do what is right *despite* the world's fads, not *because* of them. Atheists tell us to let morality evolve, but Latter-day Saints understand that God's laws don't change to fit the world's fashions and we must live them regardless of popularity.[20] Lehi's vision of the great and spacious building serves as a profound metaphor of the ridicule we must endure when the world's fashions evolve away from moral truth. We understand that "popular" does not mean "morally right" and, since we are not beholden to Darwinian fundamentalism like atheists are, we can make a distinction.

The atheist morality of "evolution" and "fashion" is easy—it lets us do whatever we feel like doing, so long as everyone else feels like doing it too. The religious morality of ontological realism is difficult—we must refrain from doing what we feel like doing, especially if everyone else feels like doing it too. God tells us what we don't want to hear, and any morality that is more than fashion would do the same. Atheist morality has no authority other than "social convention" or "history" to appeal to; religious morality has no less an authority than God Himself to appeal to.

The mere mention of God as an "authority," though, causes atheists to refer to God as a "celestial tyrant." Earthly authorities oppress and control us, they say, so why would I want to believe in a Heavenly Authority who

---

20 Invoking changes in Church policies or temple recommend interview questions doesn't prove otherwise. It merely shows that God applies His principles differently at different times or requires them in different degrees as Latter-day Saints are able to live them.

controls me as well? Scottish sprinter Eric Liddell dispelled their errone-
ous thinking easily enough in the film *Chariots of Fire*, pointing out that,
"God commands, but nobody's forcing you to obey." Asking is not controlling, so God is no more a tyrant than is a beggar asking for charity.[21]

Atheists must also realize that doing away with God doesn't do
away with the reality of authority; it only shifts the source. If there is
no God, then it's not that authority has disappeared, only that humans
have become the final authority on what is right and wrong. Whatever
humans happen to agree on—be it the correctness of slavery, genocide, or
abortion—becomes morally right. They have no final, fixed position from
which to evaluate what is moral. They are stuck deriving their morals
from social fads. Werner Heisenberg, one of the greatest scientists of the
twentieth century and a committed Christian, well pointed out this truth.

> Where no guiding ideals are left to point the way, the scale of values
> disappears and with it the meaning of our deeds and sufferings, and
> at the end can lie only negation and despair. Religion is therefore the
> foundation of ethics, and ethics the presupposition of life.[22]

Atheists often dismiss the idea of transcendent morality as dated, but
we must accept it or accept the implications of a morality that will otherwise follow. We either have moral nihilism or we have God.

4. Epistemology

The gospel also gets us past the moral-empirical problem by admitting revelation as a source of knowledge. The gospel not only teaches that
there *are* moral truths, but it also gives us a way to *know* them. "The
Spirit of Christ is given to every man, that he may know good from evil"
(Moroni 7:16), and we can know what is right and wrong through that
Spirit (as given to us or to God's prophets). Latter-day Saints, rejecting
the dogma of empiricism, have a valid path to knowledge of moral truths.

---

21 This religious misunderstanding parallels a typical political misunderstanding.
    People often err in thinking that asking and forcing are the same thing. I can
    try to persuade you to join my cause or I use power of state to force you to.
    Totalitarian societies don't make a distinction, but free societies do.

22 Heisenberg, speech before the Catholic Academy of Bavaria on acceptance of the
    Guardini Prize, March 23, 1974, quoted in Brian Nugent, *Sli na Firrine: Catholic
    Proofs of God's Existence* (Oldcastle: Corstown: 2011), 295.

While atheists are stuck without a means to know which of our natural inclinations to indulge and which to deny, Latter-day Saints have a criterion for distinguishing between different aspects of our natural dispositions—God's commandments. We agree that there are those natural inclinations (such as compassion) that we should follow and encourage and those natural inclinations (such as vengeance) that we should avoid and discourage. Our natural self is a double-edged sword, and certain elements of the natural man need to be resisted and subdued (see Mosiah 3:19), while others should be cultivated and encouraged. The gospel tells us clearly when to accede to our natural inclinations and when to rise above them. Atheism does not.

5. Agency

Morality cannot exist without choice, and the gospel also teaches the reality and fundamental importance of agency. We cannot do good if we could not have done evil, so agency is a precondition for morality. Righteousness is not true righteousness if it is not chosen (see 2 Corinthians 9:7), and material objects are hardly responsible for anything they do. A falling tree is not responsible for killing a lumberjack in an accident—it is just a natural object following the laws of physics. If a human is as much a natural object as the tree, then a human is not responsible for a murder he commits. If there is no agency, a murderer is no more responsible for a death than is the river that drowns or the lightning that strikes. We don't condemn lions for hunting zebras, ants for building hills, comets for colliding with planets, trees for falling, or rivers for flowing. They are mere materials following the laws of nature—they had no choice. If the laws of nature, rather than choice, govern our behavior, then there is no fault or praise in following those laws. We don't punish people for following the law of gravity, so how could we punish them for following the law of genetic destiny which forced them to commit a crime?

In the gospel, on the other hand, choice is fundamental, so the reality of good and evil is equally fundamental (see Genesis 3:22). Since the Fall, we have known good from evil and have had the capacity to choose between them. We are, therefore, responsible for our moral decisions. We can condemn the murderer for killing someone—he is a subject. We can't condemn the river for drowning someone—it is an object.

Materialists who deny agency and see humans as mere objects with the rest of nature are also caught in self-contradiction. Many atheists, rejecting free will, argue that we shouldn't punish criminals (in a non-deterrent way) because they are not responsible for their actions. They are just biological robots following their genetic and environmental programming and could not have done otherwise. Atheist attorney Clarence Darrow, for instance, dedicated most of his life to exonerate even guilty criminals (to the materialist, there really cannot be such a thing as guilt), arguing that their crimes were not the result of choices but of millions of years of evolution. To Darrow, suffering was real but not choice, so it made sense to do away with punishments for crimes people could never be responsible for.[23]

But in asking *us* not to punish criminals, the atheist is assuming that *we* are responsible for punishing them. The contradiction is that atheists try to persuade us that there is no moral responsibility so that we will behave in a morally responsible way. If criminals are robots who couldn't have helped their actions, then the judges, juries, and voting public who send them to prison or the electric chair are also robots who can't help their actions. Why, then, is the atheist upset about the death penalty or other harsh sentences for criminals? The atheist needs to make up her mind: either nobody is morally responsible, in which case she needs to quit lecturing us about punishing criminals, or people *are* morally responsible, in which case criminals can justly be punished for their chosen actions.

Collectively, the above five principles show why God justifies the existence of morality, but they also imply the converse: morality justifies the existence of God. We can derive morals from the reality of God, and we can derive the reality of God from morals. In other words, moral truth itself is an argument for God. We know, openly or deep down, that there are transcendent moral truths. We know that humans don't just make them up for our convenience. We know that the right thing to do is different from the popular (currently evolved) thing to do. The fundamental fact that there is moral truth disproves materialism and points to a higher being as a source of that truth. If there is no God, then there is no good; but if there is good, then there must be a god. It's not only that we need God for good, but we can find God *through* good.

We find this line of reasoning in 2 Nephi 2:13, which teaches the following:

---

23   See John A. Farrell, *Clarence Darrow: Attorney for the Damned* (NY: Vintage, 2012).

And if ye shall say there is no law, ye shall also say there is no sin. If ye shall say there is no sin, ye shall also say there is no righteousness. And if there be no righteousness there be no happiness. And if there be no righteousness nor happiness there be no punishment nor misery. And if these things are not there is no God. And if there is no God we are not, neither the earth; for there could have been no creation of things, neither to act nor to be acted upon; wherefore, all things must have vanished away.

Moral choice, the reality of moral law, and God are all bound together. God is accompanied by the good, and the God Delusion is accompanied by the Good Delusion.

INDIVIDUAL WELL-BEING

Not only are religious people generally more ethical than the nonreligious, but they also live better. People who attend church regularly and participate in worship services score higher on virtually every measure of well-being.[24] A belief in God promotes community, hope, gratitude, optimism, and a sense of purpose.[25] Recent economic research has shown that religion especially benefits the poor and minorities, enhancing their economic mobility and reducing the tragic and growing gap in income inequality.[26] "Men are that they might have joy," says Lehi in

24   See Gallup poll, accessed July 3, 2016, available at www.gallup.com/poll/145379 /Religious-Americans-Lead-Healthier-Lives; Brooks, *Gross National Happiness*; "Religion 'linked to happy life'," *BBC News*, March 18, 2008, accessed July 3, 2016, available at news.bbc.co.uk/2/hi/7302609.stm; and Arthur Brooks, "Handsome Is as Handsome Gives," *Wall Street Journal*, November 25, 2013.

25   Two friends—neuroscientist John Eccles and philosopher Karl Popper—once debated the merits of believing in immortality. Popper rejected immortality on the pragmatic grounds that it would help us value this life more if we thought it was all there was. Eccles countered that the converse was true—fear of losing this life would help us value immortality more. Most Latter-day Saints would probably agree with Eccles. Perhaps learning to appreciate immortality was one of the central reasons for us coming to earth with the certainty of eventual death. See Popper and Eccles, *The Self and Its Brain*.

26   See Jessica Shiwen Cheng and Fernando Lozano, "Religious Workers' Density and the Racial Earnings Gap," *American Economic Review* vol. 106, no. 5 (May 2016), 355–59.

2 Nephi 2:25, and study after study shows that religious people experience far more joy than the nonreligious.[27]

Religion has mental health benefits too. Sigmund Freud famously declared that religion was a neurosis of the mentally weak. The reality is the opposite: the religious have better mental health and are generally more well-adjusted than unbelievers.[28] Leeds University psychiatry professor Andrew Sims pointed out, "The advantageous effect of religious belief and spirituality on mental and physical health is one of the best-kept secrets of psychiatry, and medicine generally."[29] Lisa Miller, director of clinical psychology at Columbia University, even goes so far as to say, "It is not a matter of opinion, it is a scientific fact that there is nothing in the clinical or medical sciences as profoundly protective against the most common forms of suffering in adolescence as a strong, personal spiritual life."[30] Freud's (and Dawkins's) claim that God is a delusion for the weak-minded has been empirically falsified. The truth is exactly the opposite.

While most psychiatrists have moved on from the ideas of Freud (seeing them as highly speculative and of dubious medical value), atheists continue to use Freudianism to explain away religion. Most recently, John C. Wathey argued that religion grows out of our infantile need for coddling and affection and that prayer is a form of adult "crying" or

---

27   Alcoholics Anonymous has brought hope and peace to millions of people and there is an explicitly religious basis to its twelve-step program. Those who have benefited from AA understand that invoking a higher power gives them strength and the ability to conquer the habits that destroy lives. There is use in religion even within organizations devoted to nonreligious purposes.

28   Beauregard and O'Leary, *The Spiritual Brain*, 236, 291. Some note Utah's high rate of anti-depressant usage and argue that Mormons have worse mental health. They fail to acknowledge that the Word of Wisdom forbids the kind of self-medication through alcohol and drugs that people outside the Church turn to. If there were no Word of Wisdom, it is almost certain that anti-depressant usage would be much lower among Mormons.

29   Andrew Sims, *Is Faith Delusion? Why Religion is Good for Your Health* (London: Bloomsbury Academic, 2009), xi.

30   Miller. "The Spiritual Child: Educating the Head and Heart," address to the Wheatley Institution, Provo, UT, March 31, 2016.

"tantrum throwing."[31] Again, there is no scientific evidence for this position. Wathey, like most atheists, is simply spinning untestable narratives
about religion. The idea that religion equals infantilism is as unfounded
as the idea that the prince equals the frog—both are nice stories but have
nothing to do with science. That atheists keep returning to the largely
discredited theories of Freud shows that they are more desperate than
they let on.[32]

Social scientists Fareed Zakaria and Angus Deaton recently puzzled over why the life expectancy of working-class whites in America has
declined over the past generation, especially since we haven't seen this
same trend among other groups.[33] We solve the puzzle by realizing that
this is the American demographic that has seen the largest decline in
religiosity. The mortality, suicide, and substance abuse rates have all gone
up among the white working class in America precisely as their church
attendance has gone down.[34]

Recent studies have also confirmed that the sense of agency that religion gives is a crucial factor in happiness. When people feel that they have
no control over their lives, they become hopeless and despondent and are
much more likely to suffer from depression and anxiety. On the other
hand, those who feel they have control over their lives are better off in
difficult moments and take far more joy in their successes. The fatalism

---

31   Wathey, *Illusion of God's Presence*.

32   On Freudianism as a pseudoscience, see Karl Popper, *Conjectures and Refutations*
     (1963; London: Routledge, 2002), 44–51; also see Michael Lewis, *The Undoing
     Project* (NY: Norton, 2017), 132–33, in which he shows that Nobel Prize
     winner Daniel Kahneman and his research partner Amos Tversky came to reject
     Freudianism when a group of its practitioners only predicted a patient suicide
     after it had happened. Prior to the suicide, those same Freudians had given that
     patient a clean bill of mental health.

33   Fareed Zakaria, "GPS", *CNN*, January 3, 2016.

34   Charles Murray, *Coming Apart* (NY: Crown Forum, 2012). This book also offers
     a nice summary of many of the benefits of religious belief and participation. An
     unbeliever himself, Murray nonetheless attends Quaker worship services simply
     to try to gain some of the advantages of religion in his own life.

THE VALUE OF GOD

(or sense of being an object controlled by material forces) that comes with atheism objectively makes people worse off.[35]

So if religion is a force for social good and generally makes people happy, shouldn't atheists just be content to leave it alone? Alma made this point to Korihor over two thousand years ago:

> And now, if we do not receive anything for our labors in the church, what doth it profit us to labor in the church save it were to declare the truth, that we may have rejoicings in the joy of our brethren?
>
> Then why sayest thou that we preach unto this people to get gain, when thou, of thyself, knowest that we receive no gain? And now, believest thou that we deceive this people, that causes such joy in their hearts? (Alma 30:34–35)

We might say the same to the New Atheists today.

STEREOTYPES

What about the widespread stereotypes of religious people as ignorant, provincial, disadvantaged, poor, redneck, and bigoted, clinging to religion because they are afraid of change? Is that stereotype correct?

Actually, it is completely wrong. Economist Lee Iannacone and others have shown that the typical religious American (defined as someone who regularly attends church) is more educated and has higher income than the median American.[36] Atheists consider themselves "brights" as opposed to "dull" believers in God, but the evidence suggests they have it backward.

Although it is commonly believed that religious people are more antiscience than secularists, this is also false. For example, while the religious may be more skeptical of evolutionary science, secularists are far more skeptical of genetic science (particularly concerning male and female differences). The idea that there are no biological differences

---

35   Angela Duckworth, *Grit* (NY: Scribner, 2016), 169–73; and Brooks, *Gross National Happiness*.

36   Russ Roberts interview with Larry Iannaccone, "The Economics of Religion," *EconTalk* podcast, October 9, 2006, accessed December 16, 2015, available at www.econtalk.org/archives/2006/10/the_economics_o_7.html.

in dispositions, cognitive patterns, and physique between the sexes is antiscientific (easily falsified by observing animal behavior or infant neurology), yet this view is dominant on secular college campuses. [37] Both believers and atheists are selectively antiscience on issues that are sacred to them, but neither is more or less antiscience overall.

Some young people once reported to an LDS ecclesiastical leader that their friends were getting a little knowledge and leaving the Church. He told them that once their friends got a little more knowledge, they would return. It appears that the data bear out his claim. Similarly, physicist Werner Heisenberg said, "The first gulp from the glass of the natural sciences will turn you into an atheist, but at the bottom of the glass, God is waiting for you."[38] Francis Bacon, the founder of modern science, wrote, "It is true, that a little [science] inclineth man's mind to atheism; but depth in [science] bringeth men's minds about to religion."[39]

The secularization thesis, which says that religion declines as a society advances, has also been refuted. China, Latin America, and most African countries (and even the United States over the long term), have become *more* religious with greater technological, scientific, and educational advance.[40] The secularization thesis only applies to Western Europe in recent decades. However, nearly everywhere else on the globe, progress and religiosity have gone hand in hand.[41]

---

37   The University of Oregon even recently made it a crime (punishable by firing) to suggest otherwise. Eugene Volokh, "At the University of Oregon, no more free speech for professors on subjects such as race, religion, sexual orientation," *The Washington Post*, December 26, 2016, accessed December 28, 2016, available at www.washingtonpost.com/news/volokh-conspiracy/wp/2016/12/26/at-the-university-of-oregon-no-more-free-speech-for-professors-on-subjects-such-as-race-religion-sexual-orientation/?utm_term=.8390d0e1b5db.

38   Nugent, *Slí na Fírinne*, 295.

39   Francis Bacon, "Of Atheism," *Essays of Francis Bacon*, accessed December 15, 2016, available at www.authorama.com/essays-of-francis-bacon-17.html.

40   See Finke and Stark, *The Churching of America; and Butler, Awash in a Sea of Faith*.

41   John Micklethwait and Adrian Wooldridge, *God is Back: How the Global Revival of Faith is Changing the World* (NY: Penguin, 2009).

CONCLUSION

Atheists are reluctant to acknowledge the above facts about the connection between religion, morality, and well-being. Too many atheists would rather live in ignorance than puncture their cozy worldview in which the dull, dogmatic religious believers are pitted against the forces of intelligent, open-minded atheists. They would rather take refuge in stereotypes than confront reality.

We simply must lay to rest the false notion that religion causes net harm to society. It is based on nothing more than anecdotes and wishful thinking. The reality is that religion is good for individuals and good for society. Not only is belief in God *truthful*, but it is also *useful*. If atheists succeed in propagating the lie that belief in God is a source of evil, we will live in a far stingier, dishonest, violent, and unhappy world.

FINAL THOUGHTS

A THEIST BERTRAND RUSSELL WAS ASKED, "What will you do if you die and it turns out there is a God after all?" He replied, "I will say: 'Sir, you should have given me more evidence.'"[1] This quip well-illustrates a final, fatal weakness in the atheist position: they make everything God's responsibility, not ours. Like Laman and Lemuel, they don't bother to "ask of the Lord" but only complain that "the Lord maketh no such thing known unto us" (1 Nephi 15:8–9).

When it comes to biology, Richard Dawkins understands that he must work, strive, and proactively search out support for his theories. But when it comes to the far more important field of religion, he sits back and says, "Where's the evidence?" He expects religious results to simply appear with no effort on his part. If Dawkins approached biology the way he approaches religion, he would likely be fired from his post at Oxford and lose all credibility as a scientist. This double standard is characteristic of virtually all scientific materialists.

While atheists believe they need only wait for God to reveal Himself, the gospel teaches otherwise. We must work diligently, keep the commandments, search, ponder, pray, and find God through a long, demanding process. Is God, then, playing hide-and-seek? In a sense He is and for the same reason that children play: if none of them hid, it would defeat the very purpose of the game. Why play hide-and-seek if there is neither hiding nor seeking? Similarly, seeing God on demand would defeat the very purpose of life. In both hide-and-seek and religion, the search is the whole point.

---

1   The story is often repeated but may be apocryphal. See, for example, Tim Crane, "Mystery and Evidence," *New York Times*, September 5, 2010, accessed December 15, 2016, available at opinionator.blogs.nytimes.com/2010/09/05/mystery-and-evidence/?_r=0 .

Truman Madsen once pointed out that atheists don't find God for the same reason that bank robbers don't find policemen: they are not looking very hard. "Seek and ye shall find," the Master taught (Matthew 7:7). These words apply to finding God not only through spiritual witness but also through empirical witness in this life or the life to come. Many atheists don't seek because they don't want to find. Searching for God is one of the primary purposes of mortality, and only those who seek will find. One cannot have a true testimony without making the effort to search. The reward, unlike in children's games, is not a momentary thrill but eternal life.

As always, then, atheist arguments against God's existence stem from a fundamental misunderstanding of His nature. The atheist believes God would put no responsibility on His children for their own spiritual advancement. Atheists can't refute the true God of our worship, so they invent a false deity who should show off to unbelievers and be discoverable as scientific hypothesis. In that sense, atheists are right—God as they conceive of Him *is* a delusion. But when it comes to the real God, atheists haven't offered persuasive arguments against His existence. And since atheists have no explanation for consciousness, love, morality, meaning, order, joy, and all of the other most important aspects of our experience, their philosophy is inadequate for a full and meaningful life.

This leaves us with the conclusion that the LDS understanding of God is not only beautiful and true, but it's also robust against the assaults of atheism that have become so common in the twenty-first century. Latter-day Saints, by understanding the strengths of their own doctrine—a few of which I've emphasized above—can become more equipped to refute atheism and help others retain and strengthen their belief in God in an increasingly secular age.

APPENDIX

This appendix contains arguments against atheist morality that are more technical and complex than those in the body of the book. It's a supplement to chapter seven for those who are curious and want to engage the problems of atheist ethics in more depth and at a higher level.

RECIPROCITY

A recent atheist attempt to retain morality without God comes from the invocation of reciprocity or solidarity. It is a variation on the survival ethic and goes like this: "I altruistically donate blood, money, or service to someone else because someday I might need blood, money, or service. If I'm unselfish with others, they are more likely to be unselfish with me. Altruism advances my own interest." This reciprocity, says the atheist, stems from our sense of human solidarity—the feeling of "being in this together." We humans, as fellow travelers on this planet, must look out for each other.

Atheists claim to find support for the reciprocity ethic in evolutionary biology, which shows that certain species survive by engaging in "tit-for-tat" game theory relationships, or reciprocal altruism. Even microorganisms return help for help and harm for harm. This cooperation, biologists say, advances the survival of each organism far more than their individual efforts could. Tit-for-tat reciprocity, says the atheist, is a form of unselfishness. If it is good enough for amoeba it should be good enough for humans.

Reciprocity as a basis for morals has major problems. First, it takes us back to the "is" versus "ought" and contrary behavior problems outlined in chapter seven. Just because certain organisms *do* survive by engaging in reciprocity, this says nothing about whether we *ought* to engage in such reciprocity. That we have been programmed for cooperation says nothing about whether we should heed or reject this instinct. It's just an instinct, and we have many contradictory instincts. Figuring out which tendencies to heed and which ones to deny is the essence of ethics—evolution, as always, can give no guidance on this.

Second, while certain organisms have evolved cooperative strategies to aid their survival, others have evolved competitive survival strategies. Instead of cooperating, they defect (in game theory parlance) by returning help for harm. If some organisms survive through cooperation (altruism) and others survive by defection (selfishness), then, by the survival criterion of morality, both are equally moral.

Third, the idea that "I help others because I want others to help me" turns morals into a matter of "I want." But how can that be a sound basis for ethics? Every immoral action committed in the history of the world was done by someone who wanted it done (tyrants want to tyrannize, thieves want to steal, murderers want to murder). Why can atheists suddenly claim that wanting something makes it the right thing to do?

Fourth, the atheist says that we should help others because then they will help us and thereby advance the survival of our selfish genes. Common sense and thousands of years of human history say otherwise. Defection is at least as common among people as cooperation, and aiding the survival of others has little bearing on whether they will aid you back. Chinese peasants, European Jews, and Russian kulaks all refrained from committing genocide yet had genocide committed against them anyway. In what way did a "tit-for-tat" strategy aid their survival?

And how did reciprocity help slaves in the American South? Atheists say that we can declare slavery immoral as a self-protective strategy because if I refrain from taking a slave, then, tit-for-tat, that protects *me* from being a slave. Actual history shows that this is groundless. Africans had no means by which to enslave Europeans in the eighteenth century, and holding African-Americans as slaves had no bearing at all on whether the master himself would ever be enslaved. So how could the self-protection of reciprocity tell us whether or not slaveholding was correct? If slavery was wrong (which it was), it had to be wrong by another criterion besides "protecting myself from a similar fate" because that fate was never going to come to pass for most slaveholders.

Was it rational for European imperialists to refuse to conquer native populations because the natives would then be less likely to conquer the

Europeans? Not at all. The sad history of the Western Hemisphere shows that the *more* violence committed against the Native Americans, the *less* retaliation there was. The wiping out of Native Americans almost certainly helped perpetuate the genes of the European conquerors, but that says nothing about its moral correctness.

Fifth, cooperation is hardly the rational survival strategy that atheists make it out to be. As anyone who has examined the logic of game theory knows, choosing the non-dominated strategy of defection is usually the rational solution to the prisoner's dilemma—that is, we *should* defect rather than cooperate in such a situation. Defection is simply a rational response to a perceived payout, but that in no way makes non-cooperation "moral."[1]

We can respect the rights and freedom of others in hopes that they respect our own rights and freedom (cooperation), but we can't let survival hinge on that hope. Others may take advantage of our reciprocity and turn against us anyway (defect). This often happens and explains why there are free societies and dictatorships. The dictator has defected against the cooperative equilibrium of society simply because he can. This is a rational strategy as it enhances the survival possibilities of the dictator's selfish genes. "Defect as long as it's helps you" is the rule in game theory and nature. Solidarity is not nearly as rational, in biological terms, as the atheist wants to make it out to be.

Sixth, and finally, biological "tit-for-tat" cannot give us the principles of love and forgiveness characteristic of Judeo-Christian morality. Jesus taught, "Do unto others as *you would have* others do unto you," while tit-for-tat morality says, "Do unto others *as others do* unto you." Morality isn't only returning help for help or harm for harm, but doing what is right *regardless* of what others do. Organisms return selfishness for selfishness and harm for harm, but the gospel teaches to turn the other cheek and love unconditionally. These moral principles have no corollaries in the biological world.

---

1   Game theorists note that the more iterations of the Prisoner's Dilemma there are, the more likely cooperation becomes. This does not change the basic point here but underscores it. Sometimes cooperation aids survival, sometimes defection does. So the "rational survival strategy" can be whatever you want it to be.

HUMANISM

Many atheists try to maintain morality in a godless world by invoking humanism. The word *humanism* began as a religiously neutral term during the Renaissance, but recently it has come to refer to a particular moral stance within atheism. Humanism, says the atheist, is a worldview that takes special interest in humans and their well-being. This is an exceedingly strange worldview for a materialist to adopt. On what grounds, do the materialists justify their special interest in a particular category of material (humans) against a different batch of material (say, dirt clods)? If a clod of dirt is a random assemblage of atoms and humans are a random assemblage of atoms, why would humans have a special value that a dirt clod does not?

Humanists want to have it both ways: they try to see humans as both mere material and beings with a special status in the universe. They must make up their minds. Either we are material, or we are something higher. If we are something higher, then materialism is false. If we are not something higher, then we must stop spouting the nonsense that there is any reason to take a special interest in humans. Philosopher George Santayana, himself an atheist, pointed out this problem with humanism over a century ago and atheists have yet to successfully come to terms with it.[2]

Do atheists take a special interest in humans because they happen to belong to the human group? If so, consider that Genghis Khan took a special interest in the well-being of Mongols, Hitler took a special interest in the well-being of Germans, and all of the other monsters of history have taken a special interest in some group or another that they happened to belong to. I'm not sure how belonging to a group justifies special interest in that group.

Sometimes the atheist will try to assert humanism through a call for empathy. They say things like, "Any of us could have been born into a starving nation in Africa, so we have a moral obligation to help those Africans." It's the argument that "it could have been me" or "there but for the grace of God [who?] go I."

But by invoking empathy, materialists have snuck spirituality in through the back door. Saying, "I could have been born in Africa"

---

2   See, for example, Santayana, *Scepticism and Animal Faith* (1923; NY: Dover, 1955).

assumes an "I" independent of the body—an immaterial "self" that could have inhabited a different material vessel. Atheists claim that the self is a materialist illusion, but the argument for empathy assumes that the self is a real entity that could theoretically transmigrate to other material forms—like a spirit. The empathy case for humanism, then, rests on a belief in the existence of the soul. If I am just material, then saying I could have been another batch of material is a logical absurdity, on par with saying that this chair could have been that lake. (How, exactly, could this arrangement of atoms have been that arrangement of atoms?).

Humans intrinsically know that *we* (an immaterial self) could have been born into a different material body, so we intrinsically know that we are not material beings. The material is incidental to the self, and the self could have inhabited different material. I take it that the atheist intuitively knows that something transmaterial like a spirit resides in humans and could conceivably inhabit a different body. But this intuition, upon which the empathy argument for humanism rests, contradicts their materialism.

Also notice that atheists find themselves in contradiction by one moment proclaiming the value of humanity and the next moment proclaiming its insignificance. For instance, humanist astronomer Carl Sagan famously declared that earth was just a pale blue dot in the true scheme of things. But notice that earth is only a pale blue dot from a certain perspective. For most of us, earth constitutes a marvelous and vast reality on which the totality of our mortal experience plays out. Why is the "pale blue dot" perspective better or more true than the "earth is vast and wonderful" perspective? It's not. A chemist might see a blue dress as a compound of polymers; a teenage girl going to prom would see that blue dress in an entirely different way. Neither perspective is the right one, and the pale blue dot perspective which sees the earth and humanity as insignificant is not the "right" one either.

ABSOLUTISM

When condemning the ontological argument for morality (that morals are transcendent, real, and independent of humans), atheists often claim that moral relativism is preferable to moral absolutism because people throughout history have used absolutes to justify oppression. Stalin invoked the absolutes of Communism, Hitler invoked the absolutes of National Socialism, and white supremacist John C. Calhoun invoked the absolutes of racialism.

But notice the self-contradiction here: opponents of absolutism are simply opposing one absolute by invoking another. They criticize Calhoun's absolutes of racialism by appealing to the absolute of racial equality. Relativists criticize Hitler and Stalin's actions by appealing to the absolute moral truth that genocide is wrong. Relativists don't believe the principle of racial equality is relative; otherwise on what grounds would they oppose slavery? It's not absolutes they are against, but *false* absolutes such as racial superiority, communism, and fascism.

But don't the evils done in the name of absolutes tarnish absolutism?[3] No more than evils done in the name of science tarnish science. That Stalin believed he was practicing scientific socialism doesn't mean we should throw out the scientific method. On the contrary, abuses of science only tell us that we need to be more careful, rigorous, and humble in seeking scientific truths, and abuses of moral absolutism only tell us that we need to be more careful, rigorous, and humble in seeking moral absolutes.

The same could be said against the atheist charge that revelation is evil because many people have done great evils after claiming revelations. David Koresh, Dan Lafferty, Jim Jones, and many others have convinced people to murder by declaring they had received a revelation from God. But doing evil in the name of revelation is no different than doing evil in the name of science. A method of acquiring knowledge is not discredited by those who abuse that method.

UTILITARIANISM

Atheist utilitarians are not only in the odd position of claiming pleasure as a basis of morals but also claiming that it must be for the most people. Why? Couldn't a person define morality as that which maximizes *their own* pleasure regardless of the impact on others? Selfishness is as much programmed into us by evolution as is selflessness, so the atheist has no grounds on which to say selflessness (looking out for the greatest number) is preferable to selfishness (looking out for myself).

The "most people" criterion of morality is also problematic from the Darwinian fundamentalist paradigm that sees humans as mere animals. The atheist says that we must include all people in our calculation of "most good," but couldn't the greatest good for my own family, tribe, or nation

---

3   Dawkins makes this claim in *The God Delusion*, 323–24.

be just as valid as a basis for morals if it helps my selfish genes best survive?

And why stop with humans? If we can't stop with the greatest good for my family, tribe, or nation, why do we get to stop with my species? Isn't that as arbitrary a limit to greatest good as any other grouping of materials? Why not extend the utilitarian logic to animals, amoeba, or plants? If they are material and so are we, then why should their well-being be less important than that of humans? Is a prejudice against other species just like a prejudice against other races? If we are all mere materials, then why do we privilege one class of biological material (humans) over other classes of biological materials?

Peter Singer, the atheist Princeton philosopher, is at least consistent on this point. He recognizes that if there is no God and no soul, then we have no reason for drawing the line of the greatest good for the greatest number at humans and should include all pain-experiencing species in our calculation. Furthermore, since newborn humans haven't fully developed their sense of pleasure or pain yet, he has come out in favor of killing babies. If we can abort a viable child *in* the womb, he says, why let a mere inch of tissue—the mother's abdominal wall—deter us from killing a viable child outside the womb? The logic of materialism takes us straight to infanticide and from there to who knows what other moral abominations.

OPPOSITES

Because atheists so often claim that we can derive morality from evolution by doing what we are wired to do, it's worth looking further at more of the contradictions that emerge from this position.

Thousands of parents have sacrificed their own lives to save their children, while thousands of other parents have killed their own children to save themselves (abandoning or cannibalizing them in times of famine, for instance).[4] According to the Darwinian fundamentalist, both of these behaviors are survival strategies that selfish genes use to perpetuate themselves. Preserving your offspring at the cost of your own life would help your selfish genes survive through your children, but killing your children to save your own life would allow you to live on to further procreate and thereby perpetuate selfish genes. Should you sacrifice your

---

4   Both have been common practices in China off and on throughout history, especially to get rid of unwanted baby girls. See Jasper Becker, *Hungry Ghosts* (NY: Henry Holt, 1996).

children to save yourself, or sacrifice yourself to save your children? Every decent person knows that the latter answer is correct, but you can't get this from evolution because both behaviors evolved as survival strategies.

One man saw a child drowning in a swift current and, at great risk to his own life, jumped in to save her. Another man saw a child drowning, covered his ears to her screams, and fled the scene, leaving the child to her fate. Darwinian fundamentalists will undoubtedly come up with some far-fetched story of how the man who jumped in was following the evolutionary logic of selfish gene preservation every bit as much as the man who walked away. Even so, why do we applaud the first man as a hero and condemn the second as a coward? If evolution is our standard of morality, then both are equally praiseworthy since both equally acted to perpetuate their selfish genes.

In the "selfish gene" paradigm, the difference between heroism and cowardice is just an alternative survival strategy (the result of different evolutionary wiring). How does the fact that these behaviors evolved have any bearing on whether or not they are correct? It doesn't.

Some philosophers, such as naturalist John Dewey, say that because we are merely natural beings we should submit to our natural impulses. Others, such as Paul Elmer More, argue that the essence of morality is putting a brake on our natural inclinations. The reality is that we have so many contradictory natural inclinations that saying "follow nature" or "defy nature" does not solve anything in the moral realm.

The vast, recent literature on behavioral economics underscores this point. Such noted scholars as Daniel Kahneman, Nassim Taleb, Dan Ariely, Richard Thaler, and Cass Sunstein have identified evolved irrationalities that we humans need to consciously work against. Our tendencies to pessimism, status quo bias, sunk cost errors, and so on have an evolutionary history, say the behavioral economists, but they do great harm. We had reasons for evolving each of these irrational tendencies, but "doing what evolution has programmed us for" would mean indulging all of them. On what grounds could we follow their advice and rise above evolution's programming if submitting to evolution's programming is the essence of morality? Evolution can't be a criterion of morality because acceding to or defying it is conditional upon what evolution has programmed us to do. We must get our morals elsewhere—from God.

ABOUT THE AUTHOR

Hyrum Lewis is a visiting scholar at Stanford University and a professor of history at BYU–Idaho, where he heads up the American Foundations Team. He received a PhD in history and philosophy from the University of Southern California. Before coming to BYU–Idaho, he taught at Skidmore College in New York. He and his wife, Sundee, are the parents of four children. Professor Lewis was born in Arizona and raised in Oregon. He served as a missionary in the Chile Viña del Mar Mission.

Scan to visit

hyrumlewis.blogspot.com